Folk-Tales of Iraq

Books & Books

First English Edition Published by Books & Books Ltd 1995
© Books & Books

Books & Books Limited
223 Windmill Road
Ealing London W5 4DJ United Kingdom

British Library Cataloguing in Publication Data is available.

ISBN 1 86102 001 5

Design of cover and illustrations by Su Ann Oh.

Printed in the UK by BPC Wheatons Ltd.

Contents

Introduction

This is a collection of the folk tales from Iraq which are translated from the vernacular. It is worth pointing out that, like all folklore, that of Iraq is the product sum of all cultures that have inhabited or crossed this ancient land from the recorded history of the Sumerians up until today. Some of them may appear in slightly different versions in other cultures which serves to strengthen the idea of continuous intermarriage between cultures.

Up until the beginning of this century, story telling was part of cultural life in Iraq. Male story-tellers, known as Qassakhoon, would tell their tales in coffee-houses and female story-tellers would tell them inside the house to the women and children. Some of these stories were so exciting that they were requested to be repeated at every session. However, the art is now dead in Iraq as cinema and TV has taken over to satisfy the people's desires for adventure and excitement.

Collecting some of these stories and presenting them for the reader may help in preserving some of them. As a faithful reproduction was intended, no attempt was made to refine these tales. Due to the recurrent appearance of words such as common expressions in colloquial Arabic in Iraq and the mythological figures, a glossary is presented below to avoid the need to repeat the definition every time they appear.

It is customary for each tale to be opened with a verselet and end up with a jingle. The opening verselets have slightly different versions. For example the Muslims of Mousil, Iraq's biggest northern city, to start with:

Hnak, ma hnak	There, not there,
Ya 'ashqiin an Nabi	Oh lovers of the Prophet,
Sallu 'alaih	Pray for Him,

to which the listeners would reply:

Elf as Salat	A thousand prayers,
was salaam 'alaika	And peace upon You,
Ya rasul Allah	Oh Messenger of God.

However both Muslims and Christians in the rest of Iraq may start the tale with:

Kan ya ma kan	It was and it was not,
Wa 'ala Allahut tuklan	Our reliance is upon God.

While at the end the following jingle will be recited signalling the end of that session of adventure:

Wa lo baitna garib	Was our house near,
Ajiib il kum	I'd bring you,
Tubeg hummus we tubeg zebiib	A dish of chick peas and a dish of raisins.

Glossary

'aba is the outer garment of Arab women. It is commonly black woven of wool or silk. It is square in cut and has wide sleeves. The rich women have theirs embroided at the neck and the shoulders with gold. The use of the *'aba* has dwindled during this century. The outer garment of men is also called *'aba* whose use had dwindled except for Arabia and the Gulf.

'aza is the gathering of relatives and friends to bewail the deceased.
'araq is the hard liquor of Iraq distilled mainly from dates.

booma is Arabic for owl which in Iraq is a symbol of stupidity and ill-fortune.

chalghi is the Turkish word for the entertainment session in which a house concert for which a troupe of musicians and singers are gathered for the night.

chol (pronounced as in bowl) is the common word used by the people of Baghdad for the land outside the city. This usually means land of wilderness.

'edda is the period, according to Islamic practice, which must lapse before a woman can remarry.

deyu (fem. deywa; pl. dewat) is a rustic demon who haunts woods and desolate places.

fattahfal is the man who, in the old days, used to act as an astrologer and fortune teller.

hosh is the courtyard in traditional Iraqi-style houses, in which the rooms in the ground floor have no windows opening out onto the street but inside onto the *hosh*.

kabab is made of minced meat on skewers and grilled over charcoal by the kababchi.

mullabas are comfits wrapped in a silk handkerchief and presented to every wedding guest.

pacha is an ancient dish in Iraq. It is a stew of the feet and head of a sheep together with the cleaned and stuffed offal.

7

shenashiil are windows protruding out over the street and protected by lattices. They are built so that women can see through them without being seen.

shiniina is yoghurt shaken with water and chilled. It is a favourite drink in Iraq especially with meals.

si'luwa a water-spirit who dwells in rivers or water streams. Her body is covered with long hair, her breasts are pendant, reaching her knees, and when she wishes to suckle her children, whom she carries on her back, she throws her breasts over her shoulder. She is like a woman, but may sometimes be presented as having a fish's tail. She is fond of human flesh and human lovers.

suq is the market-place usually a covered street with booths on either side.

suq as Safafiir is the copper market-place in Baghdad.

tanoor is the Iraqi clay oven that is heated by wood burnt inside it. When it is red hot the flat rounds of Iraqi bread are plastered to the sides to bake.

Acknowledgement

The publishers would like to acknowledge with deep gratitude the contributions and assistance rendered by the people, whose names are listed below, which made the production of this book possible.

Abdul-Haq Al-Ani
Aws Al-Ani
Sami-Ali Al-Ani
Ali As-Shawwaf
A. T. Jones
Mike Layton
Majid Naji
Su-Ann Oh
Ute Pyne

THE LION'S SHEEPSKIN COAT

Abu Khumeiyis, the king of beasts, was strolling one day in the desert, when he stopped by a well for a drink. When he looked down the well, he saw a wolf sitting at the bottom. The lion wished him good day, and the wolf answered, "*Ahlan wa sahlan, ya Abu Khumeiyis*! Welcome, O Abu Khumeiyis!"

The lion asked, "*Ya Theeb*, O wolf, what are you doing down there in the bottom of the well?"

The wolf replied, "I am making a sheepskin coat."

"O wolf, it is getting so cold, and I need one too!" said the lion.

"Good, I will make you one, if you fetch me enough sheepskins!"

The lion went away and caught two lambs. He came back and threw them to the wolf. The wolf complained, "What is this? Only two lambs? How can I make a coat for a lion using only two sheepskins? I shall need at least one or two each day."

The lion came by every day and threw him a lamb or two, and asked, "Is the coat finished yet?" The wolf would answer, "Just a couple more skins before I finish it."

Finally the lion became impatient with the delays and excuses and decided not to put up with it any more. He said to the wolf, "Look,

Theeb, you better have my coat ready now, as I am getting tired of this game and will not take any more of these delays and excuses."

The wolf promised, "In two days it will definitely be completed."

When the lion came, after two days, to collect the coat, the wolf said, "Only a few stitches left. It shall be ready by tomorrow. Come early and bring a rope with you."

The next day, the lion came and threw a rope into the well and pulled upon it as he had been instructed by the wolf. As the weight was so great, the lion though that the coat must have been a fine one.

He did not know that the wolf, at the other end of the rope with a couple of the skins, had grown very fat eating the lambs which the lion had thrown to him over the days.

As soon as the wolf reached the top of the well he threw the skins at the lion and ran away before the lion realised what had happened.

It was only then that *Abu Khumeiyis* realised that he had been had!

And until this day when a person, in Baghdad, who has ordered a tailor to make him a garment and is constantly met with excuses for its delay, would say, "*Shsar, khu ma farwat seb'a*! Why so long? It isn't the lion's sheepskin coat!"

THE YOUNG SULTAN

Aku maku! There was, there was not! The Sultan was a just and noble ruler, and his people were happy, prosperous, and free. However, one day he fell ill and was nearing his death, so he sent for his three sons. When they were assembled, the Sultan spoke to the eldest, "My son, my days are numbered; I hereby decree that when I am dead, you will become the next Sultan."

The eldest, almost tearful, said, "O *Baba*, I do not want to be a Sultan. All I hope for is that you stay with us forever." The Sultan replied, "That, my son, cannot be. Now, all of you, listen to my last wish: Soon after my death, three *daraweesh* will arrive, and to them you must marry your three sisters.

Also, after one week of mourning, you must watch over my grave for three nights. Perhaps unknown to you, I have some enemies, and they may wish to hurt me after my death. They failed to injure me during my life, but I fear that they may try to dig up my body and dismember it."

The sons promised to abide by their father's wishes. The Sultan died during the night, and was buried the next day. There was great mourning in the land, and all the sons, especially the youngest, wept for their father. When the week of mourning was over, the youngest prince said to his elder brothers, "Let us not forget what our father commanded us to do. We must spend the next three nights watching over his grave."

13

The eldest said, "Brother, our father is dead....so what is the point of spending the night by his grave?" He thus declined to do what his father had wished. The youngest prince was upset by this. As night fell, he performed his prayers, and then hid behind a rock near the grave with a sword in his hand. There was a full moon that night, but at about midnight the moonlit sky suddenly darkened.

The prince looked up and saw a dark cloud, slowly descending. As it approached, he realised that this was not a cloud, but a black *deyu* on a black horse. The *deyu* landed roaring, "I could not touch you when you were alive, but now I will tear you from limb to limb!"

The *deyu* dug up the grave, and as he bent to lift the dead Sultan's body, the prince boldly came out of his hiding place, and struck at the *deyu's* neck. With a single blow he severed the head from the rest of the body. He then cut out the *deyu's* eyes and put them in his *ghutra*, head-kerchief.

The prince then refilled his father's grave, and mounted the *deyu's* black horse. He also took the *deyu's* clothes and weapons. On the way to his old nurse's house, he threw the head-kerchief into the river. He woke the old nurse, and gave her the *deyu's* effects for safekeeping, saying, "Mother, keep these for me but say nothing of this to anyone." He then returned home and went to sleep.

Early next morning a *darweesh* knocked on the palace door. The elder brothers, assuming the man was a beggar, were going to have him thrown out, but the youngest reminded them, "Brothers, have you already forgotten what our father said would happen? We must give our eldest sister to this *darweesh*." This was then done.

Later that day, the youngest prince asked his brothers to watch their father's grave with him, but they both refused. He was determined, and thus decided that despite the risk of getting killed, he would, with the help of Allah, keep a vigil at his father's grave; such was his love for his father. At nightfall he hid himself, as he had done the night before.

At midnight, the prince saw a red *deyu* in the sky and the *deyu* was slowly descending on a red horse towards the grave. The *deyu* tried to dig the Sultan's body out of the grave, as his *deyu* brother had tried the night before. The prince overcame his fear, jumped out of his hiding place and severed the *deyu's* head from his body. He then repeated what he did the night before.

The next day the second *darweesh* came and married the second princess.

At sunset the young prince again went alone to the grave and hid himself. At midnight the third *deyu* arrived on a white horse. The prince killed the *deyu*, as he had killed the *deyu's* brothers, and again he took the *deyu's* effects to his nurse's place. The next day the third *darweesh* came and took away the youngest princess.

Some time elapsed, perhaps a year, then a messenger came to the city and declared that his master, a Sultan, had three beautiful daughters. He proposed to marry his eldest, but before doing so, he insisted on testing the skills of the suitors.

The Sultan ordered that a hole be dug in to the ground, fifty cubits deep, and that his daughter be lowered into it. It was announced that the man who could raise the princess from the hole, would be able to marry her. When the two elder brother's heard the news, they decided to try their luck, however when the youngest brother suggested that he would like join them, they merely laughed at him.

15

Young men from all over the land set off to try to win the princesses. As the elder brothers saw that their younger brother was determined to join them, they relented and said, "You may take the old mare from the stable, and ride with us if you insist."

Half way along the journey, the young prince made up an excuse and rode back to his nurse's house. There he put on the clothes and armour of the black *deyu*, and mounting the black horse he flew to the country of the three princesses like a bird. When the gathering of potential suitors saw the rider they cried, "*Ya Allah*! A *deyu* has come!"

The young prince flew the horse into the hole, pulled the princess by her hand and flew away. The assembled crowd looked on with envy and anger. The prince took the princess to his old nurse's house, and there he entrusted the princess to her, "Protect her as if she were your daughter, and say nothing to a living soul." She promised to do so.

He then returned home, and when his depressed brothers returned later in the evening, weeping, he asked them, "Why are you crying?" They replied, "You would not understand. We arrived and saw a beautiful princess, but then a *deyu* descended from the sky and took her away from us."

The youngest said innocently, "Is that what happened? Come, let us have tea and you can tell me more about it." But they declined, "We are so sad that we do not want tea or food."

The youngest said, "What is the matter with you? You did not weep this much when our father died!" They replied angrily, "This princess is worth more to us than our father." The youngest son was disappointed, and he ate his supper alone.

The next morning the messenger returned and announced that the second daughter would be placed in the pit, and that she would go to the suitor who could get her out. The two elder brothers decided to go at once and try their luck again. The youngest, testing his brothers, asked them to allow him to use a better horse so that he might stand a better chance. They ridiculed him, "If you had seen what happened yesterday, you would not even try."

After they left he went directly to his old nurse's house; this time he put on the red *deyu's* clothes and armour; mounted the red horse and flew to the pit. There he pulled the princess up and flew away, as he had done the day before. He took her to his nurse for safekeeping.

He returned home to find his brothers sitting on the floor weeping. Again he asked them why they were crying, and they told him that the second princess was even prettier than the first, and that she had been abducted by a red *deyu*.

Next morning the elder princes rose early, put on their finest of clothes, and by sunrise they were on their way to try to win the third princess. The youngest prince put on the white *deyu's* clothes and armour, and mounted the white horse. Again, adding to the frustration of the bystanders, he flew through the air and pulled the princess from the pit. When he returned home, he found his elder brothers sad and weeping.

They said, "Just as before, we had no chance: a white *deyu* came down from the sky and captured the girl." The youngest said, "Do not cry, eat with me for I have good news that will surely cheer you up: I have found brides for both of you!"

After supper, the youngest prince went to his nurse's house, and brought the three maidens to the palace. He gave the eldest princess to his eldest brother, the middle princess to his other brother, but for himself, he left the youngest and loveliest of the princesses. His brothers could not believe their eyes; they kissed him, thanked him and praised him saying, "You have always been the bravest and wisest...You must become the Sultan."

After the young prince was declared Sultan, the first seven days were spent celebrating the marriage of the eldest prince; the following seven days were for the middle prince. It was then the turn of the young Sultan. In preparation, the elder women took the bride to the *hammam*: they washed the bride, put henna on her hands, and clothed her in the finest of clothes.

While the procession was on its way back to the palace, a *deyu* suddenly snatched the bride and flew away with her. Now, instead of a joyful procession as the young Sultan was expecting, he received a group of tearful women who told him what had happened. The young Sultan was overwhelmed with sorrow, but soon exclaimed, "I will find her, even if it means that I have to die."

He set off in search of his bride, and journeyed for days until he was completely exhausted, but fortunately he found some shade where he wrapped up his head and slept.

By sheer chance the young Sultan had come near to the house of his eldest sister and her husband the first *darweesh*. On that day, like on any other, his sister sent a servant to fetch some water.

When the servant reached the well, he was stunned because he saw a man sleeping by the well whose looks were astonishingly like his lady's. He forgot what he came for and ran back to tell his lady, "My lady, I saw a young man sleeping by the well who looked just like you!"

"*Hai Shloon*! How can that be!" she exclaimed, and so she put on her *'aba* and went out to see who the stranger was. As soon as she saw him she recognised him as her youngest brother, and woke him saying, "My brother, what are you doing here?"

"My bride, on her way from the *hammam* was seized by a *deyu*. I must now find her, wherever she may be." His sister cried, "My dearest brother, do not go into the *deyu's* country, as harm will come to you!" He said angrily, "I will not turn away until I have my bride back!"

He went with his sister to her house. In the evening her husband, a great *darweesh*, came home with a downcast face. His wife enquired, "O *darweesh*! Are you displeased because my brother is here?"

He answered, "No, *Wallah*, that's not why; I am happy to see him. But today I saw a beautiful girl carried away by a *deyu*, that is why I am feeling unhappy."

The young Sultan said, "That girl was to be my bride. I will search for her until I find her." The *darweesh* said, "Are you sure? The way to get her back is long and rough." The Sultan insisted, "I will either return with my wife or I will never return!"

His sister tried to persuade him, "The world is full of women. You will soon forget her!"

The *darweesh* then said, "Since you are determined to go, I will give you seven pairs of iron shoes. These shoes will last you until you find your bride."

The young Sultan put on a pair of iron shoes, thanked the couple and set off on his journey immediately. He kept wearing the same pair of shoes until they were worn out and then he would exchange them for a new pair, until finally the seventh pair were worn out. By that stage he was in a strange city.

The young Sultan walked along the main road and stopped by an old woman sitting in front of her house. After greeting her he asked her if she would have him as a guest. She replied that he would be welcome, if he did not mind the poverty of her house. In return for her kindness the young Sultan gave her a fistful of gold coins and said, "This is for looking after me."

After refreshing himself, they sat down to eat, but he then heard loud music and singing. When he enquired about the reason for these festivities, the old woman told him, "The Sultan's palace is very near by, and they are celebrating...the Sultan has in his service a *deyu* who, a few months ago, brought him a beautiful young girl. She has refused to marry him, but he has decided to marry her by force."

The young Sultan screamed, "By Allah, how dare he...that is my wife!" He told the old woman the whole story and asked her not to reveal any of it to anyone. The old woman promised the young Sultan that she would endeavour to take him to see the young woman, and that if indeed she was his wife, she would try help them escape.

The young Sultan asked anxiously, "But how will you take me to see her?" She replied "I used to be a nurse for the Sultan's family and I can therefore go in and out of the harem as I please."

A barber was called to shave the young Sultan's hair and beard, and the old woman then dressed him in women's clothes, including an

20

'aba. The two then went to the palace and the old woman informed the Sultan's mother that her daughter, pointing at the disguised young Sultan, was visiting her and very much wanted to see the new beautiful bride. They were then let into the harem, but the bride had locked her-self in her room and refused to see anybody.

However, the old woman and the disguised young Sultan knocked at the door saying, "Please open the door!" But the princess adamantly replied, "I will not and I do not want anybody to see my face!" The old woman then suggested that the young Sultan talk to the bride in their native dialect.

As soon as the bride heard the dialect, she was overwhelmed and opened the door asking, "Who are you and why are you here?" The disguised young Sultan replied with a smile, "I am your groom and I have sworn either to take you back with me or to lose my life." She screamed joyfully, "O my dear husband...But what are we to do? The Sultan is determined to marry me in two days time!"

"We shall try to escape", but he could not tell her how. All three of them stood in the room silently thinking, and then the old woman said excitedly, "There is one way. Go tonight to the seashore, and by midnight a mermaid with wings will come out of the sea. Jump on her back; bridle her, and ride her to the palace below this window. You will then both escape by flying away."

That night he went to the seashore, and waited for the mermaid. Just as the old woman had told him, a mermaid came out of the sea; he immediately seized her and flew with her to the princess's window. The princess broke the window with her shoe and jumped out onto the mermaid 's back. The mermaid then flew them away until they reached their own country.

21

The next morning the Sultan came to visit his bride, but instead found the window broken and his bride gone. He summoned the old woman and ask her for the whereabouts of her daughter, "How is it that my bride and your daughter have both vanished?" The old woman was well prepared for this question and told the Sultan that her poor daughter was innocent; the bride must have abducted her daughter against her own will. She began to lament and wail about the loss of her daughter, and so nobody suspected her anymore.

The Sultan ordered his *deyu*, "Go and bring back my wife!"

In the meantime, the young Sultan and his bride arrived in their home city to find his brothers in mourning. Since he had not returned for such a long time, they had assumed him dead.

When the brothers saw the young couple, they were overjoyed and threw away their mourning, crying, "*Al Hamdu Lillah*, Praise be to Allah! You and your wife are back! Now we must finish the *Iriss*, the wedding." There was a great feast: they slaughtered many sheep, and there was much singing and dancing.

The *deyu* flew directly to the place where he had originally found the bride, and when he arrived, he heard the music from the palace. As he entered the palace, he saw the bridegroom and his bride. However the young Sultan had put on the clothes and armour of the white *deyu*, and when the wicked *deyu* entered, the young Sultan drew his sword and killed him with a single blow.

Thus the young Sultan was free from the *deyus*, and lived with his beautiful wife, happily ever after.

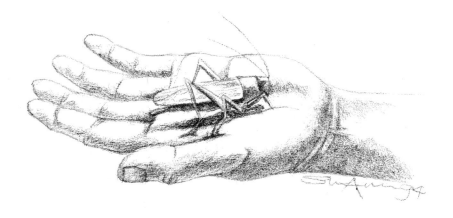

THE MAGICIAN'S WIFE

Once, in the golden age of the City of Baghdad lived a man who had very little intelligence and little interest in anything. He was very lazy and spent all his time at home doing nothing. He was married to a woman called Jarada, Locust, who was as quick-witted as her husband was dull.

Life was very hard for Jarada with her husband earning nothing. One day, exasperated she told him, "You must go out and try to find some way of earning money, at least to provide us with decent food."

"But how can I earn money?" He asked. "You know that no one will give me any work."

She replied with indignation, "Yes I know that. But have you considered setting yourself up as magician? Sit in the market place and announce to the people that you can stop the envious eye and keep off ill-fortune by writing them *hijabs*, charms."

He replied, "Magician! What are you talking about, O Wife. I can't even write. I know not the *alif* from *ya*, A from Z."

Jarada sighed, "You are really stupid. Do you think that people need to write in order to make amulets? Any scribbling on a piece of paper will be assumed to mean some secret writing; people are gullible. "

25

She gave him a pen-case and paper, and sent him off to the market-place crying that he was a *fattahfal* - a reader of secrets, a dealer in magic.

Jarada was right about how gullible people are. As it is said that even false prophets have disciples, the husband did wonders that week. He made charms against the Evil Eye, amulets against bullets, and protectors against diseases. By the end of the first week he had earned more money than he had ever earned before.

As the weeks passed his fame spread. People began to talk of the miracles at his hands and the cures he had achieved.

One fine day a woman came to him and asked, "O wise man, O *fattahfal*, can you help a woman in trouble and keep her secrets?"

"The wise always keep secrets," replied the magician.

"I am a servant in the house of the Khalifa. One day I saw the Khalifa's ring lying in his chamber, and *Iblees*, the devil, entered my heart; tempted me and I took it. Now they are looking for the ring, and I want you to consult your books and find if I will caught."

The magician looked into a book he was holding, as if to consult it. He pretended to peruse it at length, turned to the servant and told her that the stars were against her and that she should get rid of the ring

The servant asked, "How can I do that without exposing myself?" The magician looked again at his book and told her that, in order for her to save her neck, she had to put the ring in the cistern.

26

"I shall do as you ordered," the woman said in gratitude, as she paid him and bade him goodbye.

When he went home, and told Jarada about what had happened, she was pleased with the way he had handled that matter. She then put on her veil, and went to the palace.

There she met some of the women working in the palace. After exchanging the normal greetings, she began to talk about how wonderful a magician her husband was. She suggested to them that should the Khalifa consult him, he would find out from the stars where the ring was.

They rushed to tell the Khalifa's wife, who related the story to her husband, the Khalifa. The magician was summoned to appear before the Khalifa, who ordered him to validate his reputation and discover the whereabouts of the ring.

The magician opened his book, and after a little murmuring and some scribbling, he told the Khalifa, "Your majesty, the stars inform me that the ring is in the cistern."

It was as he said, and the Khalifa was so pleased with him that that he rewarded him generously.

No sooner had the magician shown his skills, than a big robbery was committed in the palace in which a chest of money and jewels was stolen. The Khalifa sent for the magician, disclosed the matter to him, and ordered him to discover where the chest was.

This was no joking matter and the magician was in trouble. He thought for a while on what he should do. Then he said, "Your majesty, this is no simple matter. I need time to consult other books and will continue my work at home."

The Khalifa, unhappy with this failure, responded, "Make sure that you succeed or else you may not have a head left on your shoulders."

The magician said confidently, "I will not fail, but I need time."

"How much time do you need to complete your task?" asked the Khalifa.

"Forty days," he replied, hoping that in forty days something would happen. In any case the only thing he could do was to buy time. The Khalifa said, "Forty days you shall have. But if you fail, your life will be forfeit."

The magician returned home very depressed and sad. Now, when the forty thieves, who had stolen the chest of treasure, heard that the king had hired the famous magician - the one who had discovered the lost ring so easily - they became very worried and disturbed.

The head of the gang decided to send one of his men to spy on the magician and to find out whether he could, indeed, track them. That night one of the thieves crept to the house, put his ear to the door and listened.

He heard the magician saying to his wife with a deep groan, "O, Jarada, one of the forty is passing!" By this, of course, he was referring to the fact that one of the forty days left in his life was coming to an end.

But the thief took the words as alluding to himself. He went back to his chief, and exclaimed worriedly, "O chief, this man knows everything! While I was hiding, he told his wife, 'One of the forty is here!' and I so I had to run away."

"We need to discover more," responded the chief, after some contemplation, and ordered that the next night another member of the gang should go and spy on the magician.

The next night another thief went to spy and heard the magician saying to his wife: "O wife, one of the forty has gone, and now another of them is passing!" The thief fled as fast as he could and reported, in fear, the words to the chief of the gang.

The chief became very upset and cried, "There seems to be little doubt that this magician knows us! And he may inform the Khalifa at any time."

The thieves, fearing for their lives, went to the magician the following night, and threw themselves at his mercy, promising to pay him a large sum of gold if he would not betray them to justice.

The magician heard them out, and considered the matter before saying, "I know each wicked one of you, but I am a man of mercy, and will do what I can not to expose you. But first you must tell me where you have hidden the chest. Nothing of the treasure must be missing."

The chief said: "Life is more precious than money. We will show you where the chest is hidden."

The next morning the magician called at the palace and informed

29

the Khalifa that the spells had worked very quickly, and that he could lead him to where the chest was hidden. He took the Khalifa to the spot which the thieves had shown him, and when the Khalifa's servants dug in that spot, the chest was found, with none of its contents missing.

The Khalifa was extremely pleased with the magician and ordered him to be given a fine house and a fixed salary. The Khalifa began to boast of the powers of his magician to all the rulers that he knew.

One day Jarada's husband was summoned to the palace, where a foreign prince was being entertained. The Khalifa presented the magician to the prince, and told the latter that he was a master of wonders: he could see through walls and through the earth. And to prove the magician's power, he asked him, "Will you tell us what I have in my closed hand?"

The magician thought of the terrible fate awaiting him if he failed and cursed the day that he had listened to his wife: He fell on his knees, crying in despair, "Jarada, caught at last, O Jarada!"

As soon as he said that, the Khalifa opened his hand, and a locust flew out!

The visiting prince, on seeing this, picked a bunch of lentils and showed his closed fist to the magician, and said, "Now figure out what is in my hand," The magician responded in desperation:

Il ydri,	"Who knows, knows
Wil ma ydri,	And who knows not
Gadhbat 'adas.	A fistful of lentils!"

30

And again he was right.

The foreign prince was amazed at the magician's powers, and rewarded him with a fistful of gold.

However, when he returned to his wife Jarada, the magician was despondent and said, "Luck has been on my side three times, but I fear that the next time fortune will forsake me. I live in constant fear that one of these days the Khalifa will set me a task I cannot perform. What shall I do, O Jarada?"

His wife advised him to feign madness in order to get away from such an awful fate.

And so the next day Jarada told the people who came to see him that Allah had afflicted her husband and that he was stricken with insanity. The news reached the Khalifa and he summoned him at once.

The "madman" was brought to the palace, raving and singing. To prove his madness, he pretended not to recognise the Khalifa, and disrespectfully held him by the sleeve and pulled him out of the room.

But as soon as they had left the room, the ceiling collapsed, destroying all that was in the room.

The Khalifa then turned to his courtiers saying: "This fellow is very wise, even in his madness! He must have been sent by Allah to save us."
The Khalifa bestowed so much on the magician that he lived, with his wife Jarada, in comfort for all the days of their life.

Wa hadhi hechaya
Nus-ha chedhba
Lo enta qarib
'Andik tubeg zebib!

And this story,
is half-lie
and if you are near,
I'd bring you a plate of raisins!

THE POOR BROTHER

Once upon a time, in the city of Baghdad there lived two brothers. One of whom, Omar, was wealthy and owned houses, land and shops. He was known to everybody in the city.

The other brother, Bekir, was a poor man who only had one shirt to wear, and sometimes barely managed a loaf of bread a day. Both brothers had a son and a daughter each.

The day came when the son of Omar wanted to marry. He said to his mother, "O Mother, it is time that I get married. I want you to find me such a beautiful bride that there is no one like her in the whole land."

His mother was very happy that her son wanted to get married, and began to look for a suitable bride. Every day she would visit the houses of the rich, famous and important families in search of a bride. She saw many girls, but none fitted her son's requirements.

After many days of her quest, some of her friends said to her, "Why do you look for a bride among strangers? Your son's cousin, the daughter of Bekir, is very beautiful. She would make a suitable wife for your son."

But the mother said, "The daughter of, Bekir, the poor man? How can you suggest that? We are ashamed of them. We don't even visit them."

They said, "You should first see her before deciding against the idea. There is no girl more beautiful than her in this whole land."

The mother was finally persuaded by her friend's argument and went to the house of her poor brother-in-law. She took with her a diamond necklace of great value which she intended to present to the chosen bride. The necklace would be a *neeshan*, the sign of engagement, just like a ring.

Poor people are usually excited at the prospects of being visited. When Bekir's wife learned that Omar's wife was coming to visit her, she was thrilled.

To make her feel as welcomed as possible, she cleaned up her house, and baked whatever delicacies she could afford.

She received her sister-in-law with the sweetest of greetings and greatly praised her son and daughter. She then served her guest with tea and *kleycha,* the traditional Iraqi biscuits.

When Omar's wife saw how beautiful the daughter was, she was astonished that such beauty existed. She didn't wait to ask her husband's opinion or inform her son, she took out the necklace and placed it around the daughter's neck as a sign of engagement.

As Omar's wife was departing the two women exchanged the most courteous of greetings and wishes as is customary in Iraq.

The merchant's wife hurried home to tell her son and husband about the beauty of the intended bride. However, when she told them the good news, they were not pleased at all, but in fact they were angered by the news. They were embarrassed by the thought of the son marrying the daughter of a poor man, and besides, what benefit would the son gain from such a marriage?

The poor man had no properties or money!

Omar's daughter said "Why, Father? What's the matter with one's brother being poor? Is money everything?"

He answered, "Of course! We don't want to have anything to do with them. It is a totally unacceptable idea."

That evening Bekir, on hearing the news from his wife, said to her, "I am certain that tomorrow morning they will come back to reclaim the necklace. I know my brother. He cares for nothing but money!"

And his son added, "When has my uncle shown the slightest interest in us? How would they ever take my sister to their home?"

However, the mother was more hopeful and took the promise of Omar's wife seriously. She could not believe that they could do such a thing as take back the necklace and call off the wedding.

The next morning, Omar's wife sent her servant to the house of Bekir. She instructed the servant to tell Bekir's wife that his mistress wanted the necklace back, as the jeweller wanted more money for it than she was willing to pay.

The poor woman was speechless. What could she say? She remembered what her husband and son had said the night before. Disillusioned, she took the necklace from her daughter's neck; put it back in its box and gave it to the servant.

Thus Omar's wife, who had been forced into this action, went to her husband and muttered, "Here, take the necklace. I am so ashamed to have to go back on my word to your brother's family."

Omar, the rich man and his son chose for the son a bride from the family of a rich merchant friend. The son had come to accept his father's opinion that money is more important than beauty.

Omar's wife went to the house of the merchant friend and discussed the marriage arrangement. She presented the same necklace to the daughter of the rich merchant. Bekir heard about the engagement and said to his wife, "Do you see how they have fooled you?"

Then Bekir's son said angrily, "My uncle and cousin have insulted and humiliated us. I can no longer walk the streets of the city and see my uncle and his son. I am leaving this city!"

His father, mother and sister pleaded with him not to leave, crying, "Do not talk like this. No shame will fall on you!" However, he was so down-hearted and depressed that he felt like killing himself. He departed and went into the desert.

Walking in the desert, he came upon some riders among whom there was a man in the guise of a *darweesh*. They greeted each other, and the *darweesh* spoke, "What does a young man like you do in the desert at this time of the night?"
The boy answered "I cannot live in Baghdad any more. I have decide to leave."

The *darweesh* said, "What is troubling you so much that you need to leave your city?"

The boy told the *darweesh* the whole story. The *darweesh* pondered and then asked, "Will you give me the hand of your sister in marriage?"

The boy replied eagerly, "Come now with me to my house. I'll arrange it for you."

Instead the *darweesh* said, "Let us make the marriage agreement now and I'll visit her every night." The boy readily agreed.

When they reached his home, his father, mother and sister rushed to meet him and all thanked Allah for bringing him back safely.

The son said to his father, "I will remain here only if you agree to give my sister in marriage to this man. If you do not agree I shall depart to a very distant land."

As they were so worried about losing their son, they agreed to the marriage and the daughter affirmed, "Yes I want to marry this *darweesh*." The marriage contract was made and the *darweesh* spent that night with his bride and left at daybreak.

Every morning, when she woke, she found fifty gold pieces under her pillow. In time the fifty increased to one hundred. The one hundred became one hundred and fifty, until a large sum was accumulated.

The *darweesh* said gently to his wife, "This money is for you and your family. Use it to buy a house; furnish it and buy goods for your family. If you need more I will increase the sum."

Bekir bought a large piece of land and built a grand house, which he furnished elegantly. Never again would they live a poor life, for the *darweesh* was providing them with a lot of gold!

Meanwhile the rich brother's family were busy preparing for their son's wedding.

The wife of Omar, the rich brother, said to her husband, "Although we didn't take your brother's daughter for our son, let us invite them to the wedding." Omar, hesitantly, agreed.

The *darweesh* told his wife "Your cousin is going to marry and when they invite you, accept their invitation and give this gold brooch as a present to the messenger. I will arrange for a beautifully decorated carriage to take you, your mother and your servants."

When the servant of the rich brother came to invite the wife of Bekir and his daughter, she couldn't find them in their old house.

She went around the city asking for the house of Bekir. When she finally got around to the neighbourhood where Bekir had his new house, she asked where the house of the poor brother was.

The neighbours said, "We don't have a poor man living here The only people who recently moved here live in this big house "

The servant went to the house and knocked at the door. It was opened by a servant. Omar's servant enquired, "Is this the house of Bekir, the poor man?"

The other servant said "This is the house of Bekir. Will you please come in."

The wife of Bekir came down and welcomed her, and asked her what she wanted. The servant said, "My mistress invites you tonight to the wedding of her son'."

Bekir's wife replied, "We shall be pleased to come."

The servant didn't fail to observe the house with its fine furnishings, and how richly dresses were the mother and her daughter. When the servant was about to go, the daughter gave her the gold brooch as a present.

The servant returned to the house of the Omar. His wife asked eagerly, "Did you invite the family of Bekir, the poor?"

The servant said, "Yes grandmother, I invited them, but you are the poor people. They are not poor anymore."

Then Omar's wife exclaimed, "What do you mean?"

The servant held out the brooch, "Here is the present they gave me after I informed them of your invitation." The wife enquired doubtfully, "Are you sure that you went to the right address?"

The servant nodded vigorously, "Yes, but Bekir, the poor man is now Bekir, the rich."

When Omar and his son came home that evening, the wife told them the story adding, "I don't know who has married the daughter of your brother, but he must be a very rich man. See what she has given as a present to the servant."

On hearing this, Omar and his son decided to postpone the wedding until they found out who had married Bekir's daughter.

That night the carriage promised by the *darweesh* arrived. On each side of the beautiful carriage sat one black slave. They knocked on the door and said "Please come. We are here to take you to the wedding." Exclaiming over the grandeur of the carriage, they stepped in and were driven to Omar's house.

When they arrived, it was the wife of the *darweesh* who went up the steps first. Omar's family looked with envy at their beautiful and finely cousin.

They rushed to greet her and cooed, "How nice to have you with us dear cousin. We have heard that you are married now. Who is the lucky husband?"

She smiled and answered, "A certain *darweesh*."

"A *darweesh*? They chorused. "Where did he come from?"

"From Allah." She said. "We don't know much about him. He comes to me at night and leaves by daybreak." On hearing this, they were very bewildered.

Then the wife of the *darweesh* looked around and asked "It seems very quiet for a wedding tonight. Where are all the guests?"

"O, Yes. We had a wedding planned for tonight". They said. "But it was postponed at the last minute until next week. But now that you are here, let us spend the evening together."

After the female relatives finished supper, the son of Omar came in, and on seeing his cousin, he was struck by her beauty. By the end of the evening, after Bekir's family had left, he told his father and mother that he wanted his cousin for a wife and not the merchant's daughter. He informed them that he was seeking to bring a case against the *darweesh* to dissolve the marriage so that he could marry his cousin.

That night the *darweesh* asked his wife if they had celebrated the wedding. His wife informed him that the wedding had been postponed and described the evening to him.

When she finished telling him about it, the *darweesh* said softly, "Tomorrow they are going to raise a case against me."

"What case are they bringing?" She enquired with surprise.

He said gently, "Your cousin wants you for a wife. He is seeking to divorce you from me. He will argue: Who is this *darweesh*? How could a girl marry him?"

She clutched his hand and whispered, "You are my soul. I would give up everything in this world for the dust under your feet. If he didn't want me first, he is not worthy of me now."

The *darweesh* looked at his lovely wife and sighed, "They will take you before the Sultan and he will give you a chance to tell him what you want."

Next morning the case was raised and the wife of the *darweesh* was taken to court.

She was asked and she responded fervently, "I don't want my cousin. He gave me a necklace one night as a sign of engagement and reclaimed it the next morning. I married this wonderful man the next morning. He has treated me well and I will remain faithful to him even though I only see him at night. I do not want my cousin. Not now, not at any time."

The Sultan ordered that the case be tried before him.

A curtain was placed between the Sultan and the *darweesh's* wife who stood next to her cousin and uncle.

The Sultan spoke slowly, "As we don't know whether that *darweesh* is a *jinni* or a human being, I am of the opinion of divorcing you from him so that you can marry your handsome young cousin."

She pleaded with him, "For the sake of Allah, No. All my uncle's family are not worth the dust beneath the feet of my husband. My life is his and with him I will stay."

The Sultan asked: "But aren't you afraid of him?"

She answered strongly, "No. Why should I be afraid of my loving and caring husband?"

"Perhaps one day he will wrong you?" Enquired the Sultan.

She answered with a clear voice, "Let him wrong me! Let him do whatever he likes to do. I will not leave him nor change my mind."

Then the Sultan asked, "Would you recognise him if you see him in the daytime?"

She nodded vigorously, "Yes, Certainly I would."

By then the curtain between them had been pulled aside a little so that she could see the Sultan's hand. The Sultan then asked, "Can you give any description of him?"

She gasped in surprise, "Well, I would say that your hand resembles his hand."

He exclaimed in surprise, "How can that be?"

She persisted, "But your hand and his hand are the same. I don't know if you can bring me a man in the daytime whose hand resembles your hand."

"Then," said the Sultan, "I must be your husband."

He drew the curtain aside completely and smiled tenderly, "I am your husband. I took you secretly for the sake of your brother who was going into exile that night. He had confidence in me when I asked him for your hand. Now you can pass judgement in this case and I will execute it. Whatever you command I will have done to your uncle and cousin at once."

Her father and her brother, who were nearby, were full of joy now that they have realised who the *darweesh* really was. Standing close by, her uncle and her cousin were trembling as they awaited the judgement she was going to pass on them.

She said, "I will not punish them. They may have done wrong to me, my father, my mother and my brother but I will not do wrong. I shall let them go free."

In shame, her uncle Omar, and his son returned to their home.

Her father and brother returned to their home full of pride and joy after having discovered the identity of their girl's husband.

Her brother puffed out his chest and said, "Now we know who the real Sultan is! They were too proud to take my sister; see how Allah has provided for her and humiliated them!"

GUMEYRA

In the City of Baghdad long ago there lived a merchant and his wife. They were blessed with two children, a boy and a girl. A day came when Baghdad was afflicted by the plague which claimed the lives of a large number of her citizens, among them the merchant and his wife, leaving the two children alone.

The girl was called Gumeyra, little moon. Since Gumeyra and her brother grew up together, they were devoted to each other. Everybody loved Gumeyra for her goodness of heart and her beauty.

They lived together in happiness for many years, the brother going to the *suq* each day to buy and to sell in his father's shop, while Gumeyra looked after the house.

A young woman, living near by, was happy to come in and assist Gumeyra with her household work and to keep her company. The two became great friends.

One day the young woman said to Gumeyra, "We have become like sisters. Why not suggest to your brother to marry me so that we may always live and be together?"

Gumeyra was delighted by this idea, and immediately informed her brother of her wish that he should marry her friend. He agreed, and a marriage contract was made, and the wedding followed.

However, no sooner had the bride entered the house than her attitude and behaviour changed. She became very jealous of Gumeyra, especially as her husband always displayed his fondness of his sister. Life became very difficult for Gumeyra, as her sister-in-law was always creating disputes and portraying Gumeyra as her enemy.

Gumeyra became a very sad girl. When the moon shone into her room at night, it comforted her and she began to talk to it, and said:

Ya gumeyr yemwenness al garayib,
Bil layl 'indi ou binnahar ghaib.

O Moon who amuses strangers
At night you are with me,
but by day you are gone.

Her sister-in-law heard her, and said to her husband, that Gumeyra had a lover, called Gumeyr, who visited her at night. When the husband refused to believe this story, his wife insisted that he should await the night and see for himself.

The next night the brother waited behind the door and listened. He heard his sister repeating what his wife had related. In a moment of extreme anger he stormed into the room, but found no body. His sister protested her innocence, but he was not in a mood to listen to her.

He blocked the window and the door with bricks leaving only a small hole through which he was to push bread and water. All that love between Gumeyra and her brother seemed to have evaporated so suddenly.

However, the angels visited Gumeyra everyday and brought her meat and vegetables. She ate well such that her health and beauty were not adversely affected by her imprisonment. If anything she became even more beautiful.

But Gumeyra was missed by all those who knew her. When the neighbours learnt of her imprisonment, they pleaded with her brother to release her. As time passed, he cooled down and came to his senses, he began to doubt his wife's tale. With all these factors working together, he let his sister out of her room.

It was now nine months since the wedding, and the wife gave birth to a boy.

One day the wife went out to the *suq*, leaving the new-born child in the care of Gumeyra. When she returned, she saw both Gumeyra and the child sleeping.

She was so blinded by her growing hate for Gumeyra and wanted so badly to get rid of her, that she took a knife and killed her own child. She then put the bloody knife beside the sleeping Gumeyra and rushed to her husband, screaming that his sister had murdered their baby.

When the brother got to the room he saw his son dead, with Gumeyra asleep and the knife beside her. Gumeyra was waken up by wailing. Her brother, who was unable to doubt his eyes, jumped upon her and tore out both her eyes, and threw her out into the street, shouting and cursing.

Gumeyra was shattered with the pain and horror she had suffered. As she had been blinded she knew not where she was going as she

47

wandered in the country. At last she stumbled on the steps of what felt like a big house. When the servants saw this misery on the doorstep, they pitied her and took her side to the lady of the house.

That lady was a *hakima,* doctor, who had treated and cured many people. When she saw Gumeyra, she felt sorry for her, and took her into her house and began to treat her.

It was not long time before Gumeyra was able to see again. As the lady saw Gumeyra to be so bright she made her a servant, then assistant and finally taught her the art of healing.

Gumeyra lived with the lady for many years. She helped the lady with her good work, until the lady passed away, leaving the house, her practice and all her possessions to Gumeyra.

In the meantime, for their wickedness to Gumeyra, Allah had afflicted her brother with blindness and his wife with leprosy.

The news reached them that there was a lady, in the city next to theirs, who had such talents in medicine that she had worked the most marvellous cures upon the sick who sought her help.

The husband and wife travelled to the city and got to the house, where Gumeyra lived. She, immediately, recognised them but they did not. She employed her skill on her brother with such dedication that she managed to cure him. When he regained his sight he saw her and recognised her.

Gumeyra said to him, "Do you believe now that I did not kill your son. How could you believe that Gumeyra, who had loved you all her life, could do any harm to you?"

He answered in shame, "I know now that you are innocent."

Then Gumeyra said to her sister-in-law, "You are a very wicked woman. So wicked that you killed your own son. I will neither cure nor kill you. Just leave us."

The wicked woman fled the city. Gumeyra and her brother returned to living their lives as they had done before the wicked woman entered it. They lived happily to a very old age.

THE GENEROUS AND THE NIGGARDLY

Once, in the city of Baghdad, lived two half-brothers. The son of the Baghdadi woman was generous but the son of the Mosuli woman was closefisted. However, both were very poor, and had little material wealth.

One day, they decided to go out into the world to try to improve their fortunes.

The generous brother said, "Let us go into the desert and beyond it to see if we can find any work. But we have to take some bread with us lest we starve to death. We should agree now that whoever runs out of food first will rely on the other to give some of his bread."

The niggardly brother agreed with him. So each one went to his mother and asked for bread to be baked as they were preparing to embark on their trip. Each mother baked some bread and gave it to her son, before they set off together into the desert.

After having travelled for a while, the generous brother consumed his bread and asked his brother to give him some of his. The niggardly brother refused and said, "I am sorry but our agreement of yesterday has lapsed. I shall not give you any of my bread."

The generous brother cried, "What is this world coming to? First I am your brother, second I am hungry and third we had an agreement. I only need a morsel!" The greedy one said, unfeelingly, "I can't spare you a crumb."

The generous one replied, "If you refuse me even a crumb, then we part here." So they parted with each one going in a different direction.

After walking all day, the generous brother became tired as night set in. He saw a cave and said to himself, "I will spend the night in this cave and Allah will be my protector from any evil." He entered the cave, and, on finding a corner, curled up and went to sleep.

When night fell, two lions entered the cave. The generous brother was woken up by their noise.

One lion said to the other, "I smell a *Beni Adam*, son of man, here." The other replied, "How can *Beni Adam* be here? No man would dare come here. It must be our smell after having just eaten a man."

On hearing the lions, the man began to tremble with terror. One of the lions said to the other, "Did you know that there is a rat in this cave, who has a hole full of gold? Every morning, at sunrise, he takes out the gold and plays with it before putting it back in the hole. If we were to kill the rat we can take all the gold".

"And what shall we do with the gold", asked the other lion.

The first lion continued, "In the town closest to us there is a Sultan whose daughter is afflicted by a *jinni,* and her father is seeking a cure. Her cure is to be bathed in the blood of a black dog. Near here there are some Bedouin with a black dog. If we purchase the dog; kill it and take its blood we can save the princess."

The second lion replied, "This is work for *Beni Adam,* not lions' work". After a little more conversation they fell asleep. The man, although terrified, had listened with great interest to what they were saying.

The man took a heavy stone in his hand and waited until dawn broke. As the sun light struck the entrance of the cave, a rat came out from a hole in the rock, dragging a tray which he placed at the mouth of the cave. He went into the hole and began to bring out pieces of gold and place them on the tray.

As the rat started to play with his gold, the man threw the stone at the rat's head and killed it instantly. He gathered the gold in his *keffiyeh,* head-kerchief, and ran from the cave as quickly as he could.

He asked for the Bedouin camp and was directed there. He went to one of the tents, entered it and sat down. He was offered some *laban,* milk, bread and *shiniina,* yoghurt drink. When he took a piece of gold and tried to pay for it he was told, "We are Arab, we do not charge our guests."

After he finished his drinks, he lay down to sleep. When he woke up the next morning, he went to look for the big black dog and saw it tied to one tent. When he enquired from its owner if he would sell it, the owner said, "No, why should I want to part with a faithful, strong dog?"

The generous man said, "I will pay a good price for it." The Bedouin shook his head, "No. I told you that I will not part with him." The man said, "You name your price and I will pay!"
"I will not sell him."

"I will give you ten gold pieces."

"*Maiseer*! It cannot be!

"Twenty."

"It cannot be." And so it went on until the generous man said, "Fifty."

The Bedouin could not resist this sum of money which he had never seen in his life, and said, "Sold! Take it quickly before I change my mind!"

The generous man gave him the gold, and took the dog. He obtained a *tunga*, clay jar, and walked into the desert. There he put the dog in a hole, killed it and let its blood flow into the *tunga*.

He travelled to the Sultan's town and walked down the streets shouting, "A healer! A healer!" The Sultan's servants, who heard him, rushed to the Sultan saying, "O Sultan a new physician has come to the town. Shall we bring him to you?"

The Sultan replied, "What use is it? I have employed so many physicians, but all failed. Why should this one be any better?"
His Wazir said, "Let this one be one more attempt. We have nothing to lose. Let us call him, and see. After all we say:

Hijaret el ma teijbeck tiffakhak
The stone that may not be pleasing can still crack your skull."

The Sultan then agreed to summon this new healer. When in his presence, the Sultan said to him, "My daughter is possessed of a

54

jinni. Can you really cure her?" The man nodded, "I will cure her, Allah willing "

The Sultan warned him, "I have had too many failed promises and will not go through this again. So I must warn you that if you do not cure her, I will cut off your head."

The man replied, "You have given me a condition. I will give you one too".

The Sultan nodded and the man continued, "If I cure your daughter, I will marry her. If I do not, you may cut my head off."

The Sultan gave his word that it shall be so.

Then the healer said, "Prepare the bath." When he asked about the princess, he was told she was chained in the *serdab*, cellar. He was taken down and left with her. She began to cry when she saw him.

The healer ordered her to rise and she did, trembling with fear. After she was taken to the bath, the healer asked to be left alone with her. He poured the dog's blood on her head, and rubbed it all over her skin, until her body was completely covered with the blood.

She sat silent for sometime and when she lifted her head she asked in bewilderment, "Who is this strange man and what is he doing here?" She then started screaming for her servants, who rushed in joyfully after hearing their names. The message that the princess was cured spread through the palace. The Wazir rushed to the Sultan to get some favour as it was he who had suggested calling the new healer.

The Sultan entered his daughter's *diwan*, and she rose to kiss his hands and feet. He was overjoyed at seeing his daughter cured.

As he sat down to talk to her about all that had happened, the healer entered his presence, and said, "Your Majesty, I have kept my part of the agreement, now it is time for you to keep yours."

"Yes", replied the Sultan, "Call the *mullah*, and let us finalise the marriage contract." The wedding followed in great rejoicing.

The Sultan felt so much joy that he crowned his son-in-law saying, "I have no son. Now you are as good as my son, and you shall rule this kingdom."

This is how Allah rewarded this generous man.

Days passed with the new Sultan reigning wisely. One morning, as he was looking out from the window, he saw a *darweesh* passing below begging for food. He immediately recognised him as his niggardly brother.

The Sultan ordered one of his servants to fetch the *darweesh*. The servant went out and called, "*Darweesh*, *Darweesh*, come here, our Sultan wants you." The *darweesh* replied, "What does a Sultan want from a *darweesh* like me?"

When he was in the presence of the Sultan, he did not recognise him. After he was offered food and drinks, the Sultan asked him if he recognised him.

The *darweesh* replied, "Your Majesty how would a poor *darweesh* like me, know you? The Sultan then asked, "Are you sure that you do not know me?" The *darweesh* shook his head, "I do not know you at all!"

The Sultan said, "I am that brother to whom you refused a morsel of bread. See how differently Allah has done for each of us." The *darweesh* fell upon his knees and pleaded with the Sultan to have mercy on him, "Do not treat me as I treated you." The Sultan replied, "Never! I would never do that!"

The *darweesh* enquired, "How did you get to where you are now? Tell me, may be I can improve myself like you." The Sultan refused to tell him about his experience, but the *darweesh* persisted.

Finally the Sultan gave in and told him his story. Then the *darweesh* said, "I will go to the lions cave and try my luck to gain riches."

The Sultan pleaded with him saying, "No my brother, do not go there! I fear evil will befall you. Now that we have found each other again, stay with me here. Enjoy life with us as I will look after you and protect you."

Although the *darweesh* pretended that he heeded his brother's advice, one day he took some food and money with him and set off to the lion's cave. He entered the cave and hid himself behind a rock.

When the lions entered the cave one of them said, "I smell *Beni Adam*!" The other said, "How could there be a man here?"
"You said that last time, but a man was here and took the treasure", answered the first lion.

So they began sniffing around the cave until they found the miserly brother hiding. One of the angry lions cried, "How shall we eat you? You deprived us of the treasure."
"No, no, it wasn't me, it was my brother."

Then the lions jumped on him and ripped him into to two halves and ate him up. That was how the greedy, niggardly, brother was rewarded.

THE BRAVE PRINCE

Fi Yom min al eyam - In a day of days!
Wa sa'a min az zaman - and an hour of time!
Allah yansur al Sultan - Allah make the Sultan victorious!

Once upon a time there was a Sultan in Baghdad who had two wives, one from Baghdad and the other from Mosul. The Baghdadi woman had two sons, but the Mosuli woman had only one. Eventually, the day came when the sons were of age, and they needed to marry. They went to their father and asked him to find wives for them.

The Sultan said to the two eldest, "Go into the courtyard and take your bows. Then shoot your arrows, and wherever your arrows fall, from that house you shall have your brides." The two sons of the Baghdadi wife obeyed their father and shot their arrows. The arrow of the eldest fell on the roof of an Emir who was living in the city. The Sultan then sent an envoy to ask for the hand of the Emir's daughter. The rites of betrothal were performed and later the eldest prince was married.

The arrow of the second prince fell on the house of the Sultan's Wazir. Again an envoy was sent to ask for the Wazir's daughter, the rites of betrothal were performed and they were then married. As for the third son, the son of the Mosuli woman, he was not asked to shoot his arrows. He was very sad, and so decided to leave the city and go out into the wilderness. He walked and walked aimlessly, until suddenly he saw at a distance a wounded lion stretched out beneath a tree.

59

The lion called out to him "*Beni Adam*! Son of man, do not fear. I will not harm you. Please, come and help me." The lion had injured a paw, and he held it out to the young prince, saying, "Cure me and I will ensure that Allah will provide for you in abundance."

The young man took the paw into his hand and saw that there was a thorn implanted in it. He pulled it out, and the pain ceased. The lion then said, "I cannot thank you enough. Pluck out three hairs from my fur and rub them together whenever you are in need. All your wishes will then be fulfilled."

The lion then took his leave and the young prince impatiently rubbed the three hairs together. Immediately three slaves appeared before him, and they spoke: "Ask of us whatever you wish, your wish is our command." The prince said to them, "Bring me a horse that can fly" and instantly a beautiful horse stood before him. He then asked for an elegant saddle and bridle for the horse, and splendid clothes for himself, and again in an instant the horse was caparisoned, and the prince finely dressed.

He cautiously mounted the horse and rode through the air, until he found himself near a city. Just outside the city he met a shepherd from whom he bought a sheep, which he slaughtered. The prince ate some of the sheep, but the paunch he placed upon his head so that he would appear bald. He then entered the city and proceeded to the Sultan's palace.

He asked the palace gardener to allow him to work in the garden. Of course the gardener agreed to the prince's offer, as the prince was willing to work without pay. One day, as the Sultan's beautiful young daughter was looking out from her window into the garden, our prince saw her and immediately rubbed the three hairs together. He asked to be transformed into a handsome man on a beautiful mare, which was how the princess saw him. She, upon seeing him, fell in love with him at once.

Some time later, the Sultan's daughters leant from the window and spoke to the gardener, "Do us a favour and tell our father, the Sultan, that we are 'marriage ripe'." The gardener replied, that being the simple gardener that he was, he could not address the Sultan on such a matter, but he would send him a message to that effect.

He then picked three melons, one over-ripe, one approaching over-ripeness, and one at its perfection. He placed them in a basket and had them delivered to the palace.

However when the Sultan saw the state of the melons, he was angry with the gardener and ordered that he should be punished for being so careless.

Fortunately, the Sultan had a wise Wazir who understood the message intended by the gardener. He explained to the Sultan the meaning of the three melons. The Sultan's anger abated, and he sent for his daughters. He gave each of his daughters an apple, and ordered that each one of them should throw her apple at the man of her choice.

The Sultan then ordered that all men of marriageable age should assemble and parade themselves below the place windows. As they paraded the eldest princess threw her apple to the Emir's son. The Sultan asked the Emir to approve his son's marriage to the eldest princess. The Emir was delighted by the request and marriage was completed within a week.

The following week a second parade was made for the middle

princess. She threw her apple to the Wazir's son. As with the eldest daughter, a marriage contract was completed and the wedding took place, with the celebrations lasting for one week.

It was then the third week, and the turn of the youngest daughter to select a husband. However this time, the procession of eligible men kept parading below the window but the princess made no decision. This went on for three days! Her ladies-in-waiting came to her and said, "There is not a man left in the city who hasn't passed by your window! What are you waiting for?"

She replied, "I have not yet seen the gardener's assistant. Why has he not paraded with the rest of the men?"

"What the bald, dirty, poor fellow!" they sneered. But when he was brought to her she threw the apple at him at once.

The Sultan was not happy, in fact he was very angry, because his daughter had refused all the wealthy noble men and instead chose this dirty, bald gardener's assistant! He thus ordered that the princess and her chosen husband should be confined to the stables.

Not long after all this, war broke out in a distant land, and the Sultan headed a large army to meet his enemies. Once the young prince heard about the battle, he left the city confines and there rubbed the three hairs together. He requested his mare, fine clothes and arms. He rushed into battle and fought better than a hundred of the Sultan's soldiers.

The Sultan wanted to know who the fearless fighter was, but nobody knew his name. The Sultan summoned this gallant warrior so as to thank him, and on seeing that the young prince was injured, he used a piece of his waist shawl to bandage the young prince's wounded hand. The Sultan wanted the young prince to stay with the army and to join them in their victorious trip back home, but our prince managed to find an excuse to leave, before the Sultan got to know his name.

Again, he rubbed the three hairs and was transferred back to the city. When the Sultan got back to his home city, he sent people everywhere to find the brave young man who had killed two thousand men, and had then disappeared so suddenly.

When all attempts failed to trace the valiant soldier, the Sultan was so saddened that he wept. He wept so much that he lost his sight, and all the doctors failed to cure him.

One old and wise doctor approached the Sultan with a cure saying, "I have read in the books of the ancients, that to restore your sight, you must obtain some lion's milk. This milk must be contained in a lion's skin, and carried on a lion cub's back, and then, if you place some of this milk in your eyes, your sight will be restored."

Now, the task was to procure the milk as prescribed. The eldest daughter's husband was the first to volunteer. The Sultan however tried to discourage him by saying that he might be killed in that pursuit. The Emir's son was adamant, and eventually the Sultan consented.

He took a bag of gold, some food, and rode his mare into the desert. He soon came to a junction of three roads and saw an old man sitting there. He asked the old man about the name and destination of each road.

The old man pointed to the first road and said, "This is the road

'Went-and-return-not', *Sadd ma Radd"*. The second road he called "Regret, *Nadamah*". The third road was the road "Goes-and-Comes Back, *Yaruh we Yiji*".

The Emir's son, on hearing that, decided to follow the 'Goes-and-Comes' road. He rode on and on until he arrived at a small town. He entered it, and being tired, stopped to rest at a coffee shop. As he entered the coffee shop he was greeted by a man saying, "*Ahlan Wa Sahlan*! Welcome. How are you?" And he continued, "I own this place, and all those who come to visit this town, come to stay here."

The Emir's son thanked him and decided to rest in the coffee shop for three days. It was on the third night that the host suggested that they play Chess. The Emir's son accepted the invite and so they sat down and began to play.

The host won the first game and the Emir's son gave him gold from his bag. The host also won the second game, and the Emir's son gave him more gold and this continued until his gold bag was empty.

The host went on to ask for the guest's horses and clothes, all but his shirt and trousers; the coffee shop owner won every time and at the end when the host had everything, and the Emir's son had nothing, the host rose up and threw his guest out into the street.

The Emir's son, in desperation, went into the *suq*, the market-place, and there asked a *pachachi* for work. The *pachachi* told the miserable young man, "I cannot afford to employ anybody. However, I do need a boy to assist me, but I can only spare a little food for wages. Will you accept?"

"Yes, I accept", said the Emir's son.

A year or more passed, without news of the Emir's son reaching the palace of his father-in-law, the blind Sultan. Everyone in the land gave him up for dead.

It was then that the second daughter's husband, the Wazir's son, came to the Sultan and said, "More than twelve months have passed and there has been no news of my brother-in-law, and your Majesty is still blind. Permit me to go in search of the lion's milk, and my brother-in-law."

The Sultan said, "No, my son, don't go. I fear for you life. You may end up like your brother-in-law. I do not want two of my daughters to become widows so early in their lives"

But the Wazir's son insisted and the Sultan eventually consented. The Wazir's son took a bag of gold with him, and he rode along the same road that the Emir's son had ridden a year before. In time he came across the old man who sat at the crossing of the three roads. The Wazir's son saluted him, and said, "Tell me the names of these roads and their destinations."

The old man repeated the description he had given to the Emir's son a year earlier. Just like his brother-in-law, the Wazir's son took the road named 'Goes-and-Comes Back', and he eventually came to the same town, and coffee shop. He was also greeted by the host, "*Ahlan Wa Sahlan*! Welcome! How was your journey? I am the owner of this humble place, and I would be very pleased if you would stay here."

The Wazir's son decided to stay at the coffee shop for a few days, during which time his horse could recuperate. He spent his time on mirth and sleep until the third night, when his host asked him, "Do you perchance play chess?"

The Wazir's son replied eagerly, "Why, yes!"

They sat and played chess until the Wazir son had lost all the gold in his bag, his horse and his clothes - all but his shirt and trousers. Like his brother-in-law, he was also thrown out of the coffee shop. Humiliated and despondent, he went into the *suq* to look for work. A *kababchi* took him as a worker, and gave him food and wages.

Back at the palace, another year had passed with no news of the two sons-in-law, and they were both given up for dead.

However, one day, the Sultan's youngest daughter said to her husband, "O husband, you were willing to fight in the war for my father, when he needed you. Now he needs you again; you must go and find my brothers-in-law and cure my father's blindness."

The young prince went to the Sultan and declared, "I will go in search of the lion's milk and I shall bring back my brothers-in-law."

The Sultan, thinking this was the bald gardener, became very angry and said "I will not have anything to do with you, you worthless idler!"

Not disheartened, the young man bade farewell to his wife and went into the desert. There he took off the sheep's paunch and rubbed the lion's hairs together.

At once the slaves appeared saying, "*Utlub We Temenna*! *Shitreed*? Ask and desire! What do you want?"

He asked for his horse, and in a blink of an eye, the horse was in front of him. He mounted the horse and flew quickly to the junction where the old man was seated. He asked the old man "What are these roads and where do they lead to?"

The old man replied, "This is *Sadd ma Radd*, and the other two are *Yaruh we Yiji* and *Nadamah*".

The youth said, "O my uncle, I will take the first."

But the old man said, "My son, do not take that road. Two youths have passed before you and they took the easier roads, but they returned not. The first road which is more dangerous will ensure that you die. You are an intelligent young man, why do you want to sacrifice yourself?" The young man told him his story from the beginning to the end.

The old man then said, "Since you are so determined, I shall tell you what you must do. When you travel along the road, you will be attacked from all sides and by all means. Whatever happens, you must never turn around, but just keep walking on. The road will end at a castle.

This castle is surrounded by a wall that has seven gates, and each of these gates will be guarded by a *deywa*. These *deywat* are ferocious and they will eat you if you try to enter through the gates. If however, you manage to remove the chewing gum from the mouth of a *deywa*, she will fall asleep. I will give you seven hairs from my beard and you must make nooses from them, so that you can remove the chewing gum from the mouths of the *deywa*.

When all the *deywat* are asleep, you can enter the castle. Then in the courtyard you will find many lionesses, but do not fear, lionesses do not harm a son of Adam, it is only lions that do that. Proceed then to kill one of the lionesses and skin it. Milk another lioness into the skin, and place the skin of milk on the back of a cub. If you survive this far, then return along the same road that took you to the castle, but remember not to turn your gaze, whatever happens to you."

The young prince then began his journey; he was struck from all sides but he kept looking straight ahead. After a great deal of suffering, he finally reached the wall of the castle. The place was exactly like the old man had described it. The young prince went to the first gate, and there he found a *deywa* that was chewing gum in order to keep awake.

The young prince made a noose by using one of the hairs from the old man's beard, and approached the *deywa* slowly. He managed to slip the noose into the *deywa's* mouth, and draw out the chewing gum. As the old man had told him, the *deywa* fell asleep instantly.

This precarious business lasted for quite a while, but soon all the *deywat* were asleep. The young prince was then able to enter the courtyard of the castle and there he saw many lionesses and their cubs. He followed the old man's instructions carefully: he killed and skinned one lioness, and he then milked another into the skin. Finally, he took a lion cub, put the skin on its back, and left the castle.

He took the only road available. This time he was struck harder and stones were hurled at him from all directions, but he still did not turn around.

He was understandably overjoyed to reach the road junction and to see the old man. The old man told the prince that his actions had shown him to be courageous and wise, and he thus foresaw happiness and prosperity.

The young prince thanked the old man for his help and kind words, and then said to him, "Uncle, I did not only come for the lion's milk, but also to find my brothers-in-law. Could you tell me which road they took?" The old man was happy to show him the road they had taken.

The young prince requested that the old man would look after the lion, while he went in search of his brothers. The old man was delighted to help.

The young prince set off on the road called 'Goes-and-Comes Back'. He soon reached the town, and the coffee shop, and there he was welcomed by the same host that had welcomed his brothers-in-law. The young man, unsuspectingly, agreed to stay at the coffee shop for a few days. Again, on the third night, the host asked his guest, "Do you play Chess?"

They played. However, this time, the host lost. They continued playing until the host lost his house and all his money. In the end the host said "I shall stake my soul." But he even lost that!

The young prince drew his sword, and said, "I am going to kill you, but you can save yourself; tell me where my brothers are!"

The host was relieved to find an opportunity to save his life, and he replied desperately, "Two young men have stayed here recently, and they played chess with me... They lost and they left... *Wallah*, by Allah, I do not know where they went!"

The young prince threw out the old coffee shop owner and locked the door. He then walked to the *suq* to look for his brothers-in-law. The young prince soon came to the *pachachi's* shop, and there he found the Emir's son, serving *pacha* to the customers. The prince then pulled out of his pocket a *mejeedy* (a coin from the Ottoman period), and gave it to the *pachachi*, asking him to send the apprentice with *pacha* to his house. "*Mamnun*! Delighted!", said the *pachachi*.

The young prince returned to his new house, with the Emir's son behind him, carrying the *pacha*. When they arrived at the house, the young prince asked his brother-in-law, "How long have you been working for?"
The Emir's son replied, "Well, must be about two years now."

The prince said, "Sit and eat with me." "I am but a *pachachi's* apprentice, that wouldn't be fitting?"

But the prince insisted that they ate together. When they finished, the prince told the Emir's son to take the empty tray to the *pachachi*, and to inform his employer that he was leaving to work for the young man who bought the *pacha*. The Emir's son was happy with anything that might take him nearer home. The Emir's son spent the evening enjoying himself, something he had almost forgotten.

The next day the prince began his search for his other brother-in-law. He searched again in the *suq* and eventually found his other brother grilling *kabab*. He ordered a plate of *kabab* to be delivered, by the assistant, to his house.

The young prince returned home with the Wazir's son behind him carrying a plate of *kabab*. When they got home the young prince sat down and invited the Wazir's son to eat with him. Although the Wazir's son thought it was unseemly for him to eat with the honourable gentleman, he relented when he recognised the Emir's son. Neither of the young men, however, recognised the young prince.

After the meal the prince asked his second brother-in-law to leave the service of the *kababchi*, and to come and work for him. The Wazir's son was pleased to do so. The three brothers-in-law then stayed together for some time.

One night, the prince asked his brothers-in-law for their life story, and they told him about their adventures and their quest. When they had finished telling the prince about their search for lion's milk, he promised them that if they left before him, he would follow them with the lion's milk.

The next morning the two brothers-in-law set out on foot, while the prince flew directly to the junction where the old man was waiting with the lion. The prince thanked the old man again, and taking the lion with him, he rode into the desert.

After some distance, he rubbed the three hairs and summoned the three slaves. This time he requested a tent, with servants and soldiers.

Instantly, all that was before him. He then diluted some of the lioness's milk with water, and put it in a bottle. When his brothers-in-law arrived, some days later, he asked for them to be brought into his tent.

The travel weary men entered the tent and saluted the prince, and he said to them, " As I promised you, I have some lion's milk for you. I will give you this bottle, on the one condition that you let me put my seal on to your backsides."

They answered adamantly, "Never! That is a shame we cannot live with!"
He replied calmly, "Then you must go back empty-handed."

The young men thought that as long as they kept it a secret, nobody in the city would ever know about their humiliation, and thus they consented to having the seal on their backsides. With the seals on their backsides, and the bottle of lion's milk, the young men departed. After travelling for days, they returned to their city.

When it became widely known that they had returned, there was music and great celebration. They went to the palace of their father-in-law who was overjoyed to have them back safely, after he had given them up for dead.

They fabricated a wonderful story about how they had obtained the lioness's milk. The king tried a drop of milk in his eye, and the whole court stood silently awaiting to see the effect.

However, to everyone's disappointment, the Sultan's sight was not restored.

The young prince, in the meantime arrived in the city, wearing the sheep's paunch over his head, and the lion's cub beside him. His wife was overjoyed to meet him, and told him that it was time to tell her father everything.

The young prince, looking like the gardener, went to see the Wazir and asked to see the Sultan, because he had the cure for the King's blindness. The Wazir told him that since his brothers-in-law had already brought lion's milk, and it was of no use, he was denied entry.

The young prince was determined to go into the palace anyway. He rubbed the three hairs and transformed into the handsome man he really was, and he entered the audience room with the lion's cub by his side. He administered one drop into each eye and waited; soon enough, the Sultan exclaimed in disbelief, "*Allahu Akbar*! Allah is great! I can see again!"

The Sultan could then see as clearly as he had done before going blind. He was beside himself with joy.

The Sultan asked, "Where are you from, and how did you obtain this milk?"

The young prince answered, "I am the husband of your youngest daughter, I am the gardener's apprentice!" He then continued to tell the Sultan the whole story, from beginning to end. He even told of how he had diluted the milk before giving it to his brothers-in-law. "If you doubt me, take a look at their backsides!", he told the Sultan. "I am also the warrior who fought in your army, and here is the piece of shawl with which you bandaged my wounded hand."

The king was indeed very happy, and cried, "Not only has my sight been restored, but you have come back. Forgive me for the hardship I caused you by making you live in the stables".

The Sultan then ordered that a festival be held, and it was the greatest event anyone had ever seen in the land. It was then that the Sultan took off his crown and placed it on the young prince's head, saying "Indeed, you are courageous and wise."

Thus, the young prince became Sultan, and ruled with justice until the end of his days.

And so ends the story of the young prince.

THE TWO BROTHERS

Once upon a time there lived in the town of Mosul a poor woodcutter. One day his son asked to be taken along; the father agreed and they set out together for the woods.

In the woods the father chopped trees while the son wandered around. At one point the son saw a beautiful bird fly off and so he went to the place where the bird had been sitting; to his astonishment he found a large egg. He took the egg to his father who said, "Keep it with you until we return home, then we shall sell it."

On their way home from the woods, they came to the *suq* where they met a trader. When they asked him if he would buy the egg, the trader seemed agreeable and asked for the price.

The woodcutter, having no idea about the value of the egg, said "You set the price."

"I offer you a thousand piasters" replied the trader, and they agreed.

It turned out that the egg contained a gem, and so from then on father and son went into the woods every day, collected an egg and sold it.

One day, when they were in the woods again, they decided to catch the bird which laid these eggs and take it home.

Even at their home the bird continued laying one egg a day, and the trader regularly came to collect this. The poor man was paid for each egg and accumulated money and became extremely rich.

The woodcutter then decided to go on a pilgrimage to thank Allah for his blessings.

He told the trader that he should leave two thousand piasters at his house every day, and in return collect an egg. The trader agreed and the woodcutter set off for Mecca.

The trader continued to come to the woodcutter's house every day, bringing two thousand piasters and collecting an egg.

However, one day, when the trader came to the house, the woodcutter's wife said to him, "My husband has been away for so long. Come and sleep with me tonight."

The trader thought to himself and replied, "If you will have the bird killed for me, I stay with you."

This she promised and instructed the slave girl to kill the bird and prepare it for a meal. While the woodcutter's wife was having a bath, it so chanced that her two sons went into the kitchen and spoke to the slave girl, "We are hungry. Have you anything for us to eat?"

"All I can give you is the head and the heart of this bird". Thus she gave one of them the head and the other the heart, and they went away, quite satisfied, to eat what she had given them.

The trader arrived at the house a short time later and demanded to be given the head and the heart of the bird. When the slave girl was asked about this, she confessed to having given these two pieces to the boys.

The trader then said, "I do not wish to eat the meat of the bird, and I shall not touch you until you bring me the head and heart of the bird."

The woman spoke fiercely to the slave-girl, "When my two sons come in to the house; bring them into this room; kill them; then remove the head and heart of the bird from their stomachs and take them to the trader to eat. Only then will he take me into his embrace tonight."

However, when the boys came in from the street, the slave girl warned them, "Your mother is planning to have you killed in order to retrieve the bird's head and heart from your stomachs, thus to entice the trader to sleep with her tonight."

The boys enquired of the girl, "What are we to do?"

"Come", she said, "Each of you take a horse and a pouch full of money and ride farther away."

They followed her advice and the slave girl fetched them a horse and a pouch of money each. They mounted their horses, and rode out of town.

The trader returned to the woodcutter's wife asking her, "Where is the head and the heart of the bird?" She replied, "Come in and sit down. Let us wait, when the boys come in from the street, the slave girl will kill them and give you what you desire." But he replied insistently, "I do not want to sit with you until I see the head and the heart of the bird before me."

She called to the slave girl, "Have the boys not returned yet?" The slave-girl shook her head.

Night fell and the trader waited. As the boys failed to return, their mother engaged the town crier to call out throughout the town, "Has anyone seen the boys of the woodcutter?" One man came forward and reported that he had seen them travel along the road leading out of town.

Hearing this, the woman and the trader went off to try to find the boys, and so they travelled from place to place in their search for them.

Meanwhile the boys, travel-weary, reached Istanbul. On the day of their arrival the Sultan of Istanbul had died and a bird was released: He on whose head the bird would settle, was to become the new Sultan of Istanbul.

The bird settled on the head of the boy who had eaten the slaughtered bird's head. The people of Istanbul declared their displeasure, as this was a stranger and could not possibly be declared Sultan. The people took the boy to a hiding place and released the bird again the next day. However, once again the bird settled on the same boy's head.

Seeing this, the people thought that this had to be a miracle and so decided to declare the young stranger as the new Sultan of Istanbul. His brother - who had eaten the bird's heart - on the other hand, found five hundred piasters under his pillow every day as he woke.

Some time after all this had taken place, the trader and the woman too arrived in Istanbul.

The Sultan met the trader there and asked him what the purpose of his visit was

"I have come to travel in this country with my wife."

The Sultan cried, "You hypocrite! Why do you lie?"

"How so?" The trader stunned, "I am not lying."

The Sultan then had the woman called to him and asked her the purpose of her journey. "I am looking for my children whom I have not seen for five months," she replied.

"And when you find them, will you recognise them again?" He asked. "But of course!" she answered indignantly.

The Sultan had one of his servants give the woman shelter in his house, but the trader was placed in a special room.

The following day, the Sultan assembled his councillors and had the two brought before them. Again he asked the trader, "What is the reason for your journey? Tell me the truth or I will have you beheaded."

The trader burst out crying and fell on his knees, "This woman and I are looking for her sons, because one of them ate the head and the other the heart of a bird."

Following this, the woman was brought before them and told, "Tell me the truth or I will have you beheaded."

"I am looking for my sons," she hesitated, "at home we had a bird which we had slaughtered, one of my sons ate the head and the other the heart of the bird."

The Sultan then asked, "If you find your sons, what will you do with them?"

Her voice hardened, "I will kill them in order to retrieve the head and the heart of the bird from their stomachs."

Upon this the Sultan stood up and ordered, "This one here, my mother, is to be executed, but the trader is to be crucified!"

In the meantime the father had returned home from his pilgrimage, and only finding the slave girl at home, asked her, "Where is my wife?" She told him that she didn't know.

"And the bird?"

"Your wife asked me to slaughter it and then she left, I do not know where to."

Learning this, the man sold his house and chattels and set out, together with the slave girl, on a journey to find his wife and sons.

Thus they, too, came to Istanbul. There they strolled through the bazaar. One day the Sultan saw his father in the bazaar and ordered his personal servant to bring him to his home that night.

The servant followed the man and told him, "The Sultan requests you to come to his palace tonight." The man refused to do so and the servant returned to the Sultan and reported this to him. The

Sultan ordered his servant to go a second time. The servant obeyed and this time returned with the man.

"Why have you come here?" the Sultan asked.

"I am looking for my children and my wife," the man replied.

"When you come across your children, will you he able to recognise them?" "But of course!" the man replied indignantly.

"Do you know of any special features by which to recognise them?"

"Yes, my eldest son has a mole on his shoulder and the younger one on his left hand."

Hearing this the Sultan pulled his robe down from his shoulder exposing the mole, "Indeed, you are my son," exclaimed the father.

Following this the younger son came in and showed his mole, "Yes, truly, you are my children. But where is your mother?", the man asked.

"We had her executed!" they replied.

On the following day the father suggested to the Sultan that wives should be found for him and the younger son, but they retorted, "We do not wish to be married off. You take the place as Sultan, and we shall go on our travels to find wives for ourselves."

The next day their father took over as Sultan and the young men set off. They mounted their horses and went their separate ways.

The eldest son passed through a desert, where he spotted a gazelle which he chased. He tried to catch her first from one side then from another but did not succeed in trapping her. Soon evening fell and the gazelle was still sprinting in front of him, allowing him to get close to her.

Night fell and the gazelle spoke, "Young prince, come with me. I will take you to our home."

"Where is your home?" he asked.
"Nearby," she replied.

He followed her and when they arrived, she called out to her mother, "A prince has come to visit us."

The mother came out, saying, "Welcome to the prince!"

Then a sheep was slaughtered. When the prince had finished his meal, the mother asked, "What is the purpose of your travels through the steppes?"

He replied, "I have come to ask for your daughter to become my brother's wife, according to the law of God and that of his prophet."

The woman said, "My daughter is the daughter of the king of Persia and you are the son of the Sultan of Istanbul. Go to your father and tell him to come here with his entourage and ask for my daughter's hand in marriage."

The following day the prince went home to his father. His father asked where he had been. "I went to find a wife for my brother", he replied.

"But where is your brother?" the father enquired.

"I know nothing of him," he replied.

"In that case, go out and look for him," ordered the father.

Thus, he left and looked for his brother. Along the way, he came across him. The young brother asked, "Where have you been?"

"I went to find a wife for you," the older brother replied.
"Who is to be my bride?" Asked the younger curiously.

"The daughter of the King of Persia."

The other said, "I too have found a bride for you."

"And who is she?" he asked. "The daughter of the Indian Emperor."

They returned to their father and told him, "If you wish us to be married, then ask for the hands of our brides. One is the daughter of the Indian Emperor and the other the daughter of the King of Persia." Their father sent a letter to the Indian Emperor asking him to give his daughter in marriage to his eldest son, according to God's law, and one to the King of Persia, requesting the hand of his daughter in marriage to his younger son. But both sent negative replies.

The Sultan suggested to his sons they might look elsewhere for wives, but they refused to do so.

So the Sultan assembled an army against the Indian Emperor in order to take his daughter by force, and a war was started between the two. After four months of war, both parties returned to their own countries.

The older prince, however, went off to visit the Indian Emperor. Once there, he placed a sword against his own neck and said, "I have come here and if you want to kill me, please do so. But if you will give me your daughter in marriage instead, that too is at your discretion!"

The Emperor replied, "As you have come here in person, I have no choice but to demand that you give me forty loads of gold, forty gazelles, forty hunting dogs and two lions. Then I will consent to let you take my daughter as your wife." Following this the young man returned to his father and reported all the Emperor's demands.

The father replied, "I do not know how to obtain the gazelles and the lions." But his son suggested that he would go to the King of Persia and beg him to provide the gazelles and the lions.

Thus the two sons set out on their journey to the King of Persia.

Having arrived there, they said to him, "We have come to ask you for your daughter's hand in marriage, according to God's law and that of his Prophet. We, in return will do anything you may desire."

The King of Persia replied, "Now that you have come to my abode, you leave me no choice but I demand of you forty loads of gold and forty mares, then I will give you my daughter."

The two agreed to this condition and immediately returned to their father, begging him to give them forty loads of gold each and forty mares, so they might go and collect the daughter of the King of Persia.

Their father did as they asked and they went on their way again. The wedding was arranged and the woman collected. One of the princes remained behind with the King and when asked why he was not leaving, the reply was, "I do not want to leave."

"But why?" asked the King.

"I desire that you give me forty gazelles, forty hunting dogs and two lions!"

"Whatever for?" asked the King.

"I want to take them to the Indian Emperor as a present, in return for a wife."

The King ordered forty gazelles, forty hunting dogs and two lions to be caught. The prince received them, took forty loads of gold and went on his way to the Emperor of India.

The wedding was arranged and he took the Emperor's daughter home with him. Thus, both brothers had their wishes granted.

THE LAUGHING FISH

Once upon a time, there ruled a Sultan who had been foretold that a daughter would bring him shame. On hearing this, he decided to kill every baby girl his wife gave birth to.

One day while his Wazir was riding his mare, he passed five or six boys playing knucklebones in the road. The mare was startled by the boy's noise and the Wazir clapped his legs very hard against her sides.

One of the boys cried, "Shame on you, O, Unbeliever! Why do you treat this helpless creature like this?"

"Is it any of your business?" Asked the Wazir. The boy answered, "This mare will give birth to a foal, which would be worth a treasure had you not blinded her in one eye by that blow." The Wazir thought to himself, "How did this boy know that my mare is expecting a foal?"

Some time later the mare gave birth to a foal, blind in its right eye. The Wazir said to his wife, "What a puzzling and fascinating boy he was. He told me that my mare will bring forth a foal blind in one eye!"

"There are many clever boys in this world," his wife replied. The Wazir continued, "True, but how did he know that the foal would be blind in one eye? It sounds like magic."

The Sultan's wife became pregnant again. She was worried that if she gave birth to a girl the Sultan would kill her again. She decided to go to him and beg him to spare her life.

She went to her husband and pleaded with him saying, "In the name of Allah I beg you that if this time I should give birth to a girl to spare her life". After pleading for a long time the Sultan relented and agreed not to kill the next girl born to them.

In due time the woman gave birth to a girl. She brought her to the Sultan and reminded him of his promise. He, in turn, kept his promise, but took her from her mother, and placed her in the care of a wet-nurse and kept them in a house next to his palace.

No man was allowed in and the child was not allowed outside it. However, in order that messages and food could be carried in and out he ordered the blacksmith to design *adami yashtughil bil yai*, a man of iron worked by springs. This automatic man would be wound like a clock and would pass between the Sultan's castle and the house where the child was being kept.

The child grew up and reached the age of fourteen. Soon after the wet-nurse left her, and she was taught by female teachers to read and write but she never left the house. To occupy herself she wrote a diary of all events that she came to know about. By now she had reached the age of twenty.

The Sultan was fond of eating fish and had hired a fisherman, whose duty it was to catch fresh fish for the Sultan every day. The fisherman was allowed to sell the fish he caught over and above the Sultan's needs. One bad day the fisherman failed to catch any fish despite the fact that he had cast his net many times into the sea. He became worried that the Sultan would become angry and that danger would befall him.

At last he drew the net and found two medium sized fish. He was delighted for having been saved from the Sultan's wrath. As he was examining the decorated scales of the fish, the fish laughed. He could not hide his astonishment, and said to himself, "These astonishing fish must be presented to the Sultan, at once."

When he entered the Sultan's presence, he explained, "I tried all night to catch fish but only managed this pair. I have never seen anything like them. These are laughing fish. I have brought them for your Majesty."

The Sultan ordered a basin filled with water be brought to him and had the fish thrown into it. Immediately the fish began to swim about and laugh. The Sultan said, "This is indeed strange! I will send them to my daughter to amuse her!" He ordered the iron-man to be brought; and had it wound up and placed the fish in its arms. On top of the fish he put a note telling his daughter to enjoy the company of this marvellous fish. The iron-man was dispatched to the presence of the young princess.

After she had read the note, she ordered a bowl of water and threw the fish into it. Immediately the fish began to swim about and laugh. The girl was puzzled and wrote to her father, "Oh, *Baba*, thank you for this amusing fish, but can you tell me why do they laugh?"

The Sultan knew not why they laughed. He summoned his Wazir and asked him for an explanation, but the Wazir was no more enlightened than the Sultan. Then the Sultan said, "I will give you three days to come up with an answer or you will lose your job and maybe even your head."

The Wazir became depressed and worried when he heard these words. His wife enquired about his problem. When he told her about his predicament she consoled him, saying, "Allah is eternally merciful. If you enquire you may find someone who can explain the meaning of the laughing fish."

The Wazir consulted all the learned men he knew but they all failed him. By the evening of the third day the Wazir sat down and began to cry fearing his end was near. Suddenly his wife said, "I have an idea. You have forgotten about the clever young boy who told you about the blind foal. Why not ask him?" The Wazir said, "How very true! I have not asked him." She instructed him to, "Go on, go and seek him."

After finding the house where the boy lived he knocked on the door and asked the mother for her son. As soon as the son came down he recognised the Wazir.

The Wazir told him the story of the fish and the demand of the Sultan for an explanation. The Wazir asked beseechingly, "If you will help me to save my head, I will make you a rich boy."

The boy said, "This is a simple matter. There is nothing to it." The Wazir exclaimed, "Tell me then!" The boy replied gently, "No, I cannot tell anybody but the Sultan himself. If you take me to him I will tell him the reason why the fish laugh."

The Wazir said, "Good. Early tomorrow I will come and fetch you, and we will go together to the palace."

Thus it was, and the Wazir and the boy went to the Sultan's palace the next morning. The Wazir brought the boy into the presence of the Sultan and said, " Majesty, This boy believes he knows the secret of the laughing fish but will only tell it to you."

The Sultan looked at the boy and asked, "Do you know why the fish laugh?" The boy nodded, "I do, but I will not tell you." "Why not?" Asked the Sultan.

The boy replied, "I will only tell your daughter." The Sultan looked at the boy, and thought to himself, "This boy is no grown man. I will let him go to my daughter."

Thereafter he called for the iron-man, and told the boy to get upon it and then the iron-man passed from the Sultan's palace to the daughter's house, and with him a note to tell her who the boy was.

The boy asked, "What do you want of me?" The princess said, "I would like to know why the fish laugh." The boy warned, "If I tell you, you will regret it."

After she insisted that she would not regret it, the boy said, "Today I will tell you a short story, and tomorrow, if you still insist, I will tell you the meaning of the laughing fish."

The boy began, "There was once a falconer who kept his falcon on his wrist day and night. One hot summer's day, while out hawking, he became thirsty. He searched for water but found none. Then he came to a high rock, and saw water drops falling from the top of the rock. He put a cup and watched as water drops filled the cup. Before the cup was full the falcon flapped its wings upsetting the cup and spilling its contents.

The man set the cup again and waited for it to gather enough for him to quench his thirst. Again the flacon flapped its wings and the cup overturned. When the third attempt ended like the previous two, the falconer was furious; caught the bird by its neck and hurled it violently to the ground where it died instantly.

Feeling guilty and sorry the falconer began to wonder why the bird had overturned the cup three times. He decided to go up the rock in order to see the source of the water. When he got to the top of the rock he saw a serpent panting with a mouth wide upon and the venom from it running down from the rock. Not even repentance would help him. So if I were to tell you why the fish laughed, you too would repent like the falconer!" She replied, "No, I will not repent."

The boy bid her peace and said, "It is enough for today. Tomorrow I will return and may tell you why the fish laughed." He went away, and the girl sent a note to her father informing him that the boy had left. The Sultan asked, "Did he tell you why the fish laughed?" "No", She replied, "But tomorrow he will!"

Then came the second day, and the boy reached the princess, like the day before, on the iron man. He asked again, "What do you want from me?" She replied, "to tell me why the fish laughed." He said, "But if I tell you, you will regret it."

She said, "No, I shall not regret it!"

He said, "Let me but tell you another small story, and tomorrow I will tell you the secret of the laughing fish."

"Tell me the story," she said.

The boy said, "There was once a man who, although married for ten years, had no children. At last, Allah blessed him and his wife with a son. This boy filled their lives with joy. This couple also had a dog called Jak, who was very attached to the boy.

One day the woman went to the public bath and left her husband with the boy and the dog. The husband decided to sit by the door waiting for his wife and left the dog rocking the boy's cradle.

There came a serpent, that coiled itself around the cradle and tried to bite the baby. Jak jumped on it; fought with it and killed it. He stretched it out dead by the cradle, and went back to rocking it.

When the woman returned from the bath, Jak, on hearing her voice, rushed to meet her. As she saw Jak's face covered with blood, she screamed to her husband. "See the blood on his face. He must have killed our son." The man drew out his dagger and killed the dog.

As they rushed upstairs, they found the dead serpent stretched out by the cradle, and the cradle was still rocking with the boy joyful in it. Do you think the man and his wife repented?" He asked her.

"They must have repented." She answered.

He nodded, "So if I tell you why the fish laugh you too will repent bitterly."

She insisted, "Never, I will not repent!"

The boy sighed, "Not today, but tomorrow, I will tell you. But you must assemble your father, his ministers, and all his court before I will tell you.".

On his way back the Sultan asked him, "Did you tell my daughter why the fish laughed?" The boy shook his head, "No, but I shall tell her tomorrow in your presence."

The next day, the Sultan, assembled his advisers, his court and the *quadhis* in the *diwan* with the princess seated on a couch in their midst. When the boy arrived, the Sultan said, "Speak, my son, everybody is here."

The boy said, "For the last two days I have told your daughter parables showing her that she will repent if I told her the secret of the laughing fish, but she insisted that she would not. Now I will show you how you will all regret it."

They all answered, "Why should we regret it?"

To the princess he turned and asked her, "For the last time are you sure that you will not regret it?" She answered confidently, "I am."

Then he said to her, "Rise, then!" The princess said, "I have repented!" and remained seated. The boy insisted, "That is no good!

You must rise," and she did reluctantly.

Next the boy ordered that the couch be lifted and the carpet under it be removed. Then he ordered that the marble slab beneath it be also removed. Below it there were steps leading into the cellar. They went down the steps into the cellar to find forty men gathered there.

Then the boy explained, "The fish laughed at the intelligence of the Sultan, who thought that shutting his daughter up would protect her from evil. She, in the meantime, received, nightly, these forty men, who came in from the desert and made love to her."

The Sultan lowered his head in shame and called his executioner, ordering him to cut off his daughter's head.

He called the boy and pronounced, "You are so clever that I will take you as a son, and you shall inherit all that I have!" And he took off his crown and put it upon the boy's head.

THE FARMER'S DONKEY

Once, in a village in the beautiful mountains of the north of Iraq, there lived a simple-minded Kurdish farmer who owned a tobacco plantation. He had a number of farm animals, among which was a one-eyed donkey. One day he remembered that an *'Eed*, a feast day, was fast approaching and realised that he needed provisions to prepare for it. So he loaded up the donkey with tobacco and led him out of the village.

Once on the road, he ordered the donkey, "Go to Mosul, to my grocer, you know him, and tell him: My master sends his greetings and asks you to sell what I bear on my back, and buy for him all that he needs for the feast; he is very busy and could not come himself, so he has sent me."

As the donkey nodded his head to all that his master told him, the farmer thought the donkey was saying "yes" and that he understood his instructions. He gave him two or three strokes with a stick and yelled, "Now go!" The donkey went on his way down the mountain, and when a dishonest passer-by spotted him, unaccompanied on the road, he led the donkey and the load to his own house.

The farmer waited for three days, and when his donkey did not return, he said to his wife, "He has found sweets in Mosul and is gorging himself. He will not come back until he has spent all the money on candy."

"This donkey is insolent," the farmer continued, "the feast is almost upon us and he delays coming home. I will go to Mosul and look for him and see what he is doing all this time". Thus saying, he started out for Mosul.

He reached Mosul and went to the shop of the grocer and asked him, "Why have you delayed my donkey all this time? It is now four days since I sent him to you. You know the feast is upon us, and it is your fault that I have gone to the trouble of coming here myself. You know very well that he has found sweets in Mosul and does not feel like returning home".

When the grocer realised what a simpleton the farmer was, he replied, "My friend, on the first day of your donkey's arrival, I attended to your orders and bought everything you instructed me to. Afterwards I led your donkey out to the far side of the bridge outside town, but yesterday I heard from people arriving from Baghdad that they had seen him there; what was I to do? If you like, go to Baghdad and look for him there - that is where he is".

The farmer took up his staff and followed the road to Baghdad. When he arrived there he looked for his donkey and asked people about him. At last, a passer-by with a sense of humour, told him that his donkey had become a judge in Baghdad.

The farmer, believing this story, started looking for the house of the judge. At length, he found the house and entered its courtyard. He peered through the window and saw the judge and his court officials holding a hearing. Now it happened that the judge was one-eyed, just as the farmer's donkey was, so the farmer was convinced that the judge was indeed his donkey. He left the courtyard and went to the market to buy grain which he put in his pockets and returned to the house of the judge. He went to the window and opened his pockets to show the grain to his 'donkey'.

The judge and his officials were, however, engrossed in their business and took no notice of the farmer. The farmer tried to entice the "donkey" with the grain, but to no avail!

Then, it being Friday, the judge rose to climb the minaret to call to mid-day prayer. The farmer ran after him with his stick in his hand. Just as the judge called "God is great", the farmer brought his stick forward and thrashed him two or three times, while calling, "You damned creature! Where did I send you to, and where did you go? You have delayed me, even though you know the feast is upon us, and now you are here in order to scream! Could you not have done the same from the mountains? Now come down, and walk in front of me; we are going home!".

The judge called, "Mercy, what are you doing? Are you mad? What do you want from me?"

"So you want to rebel against me?" the farmer replied, "go on forward: back to the mountains, I will teach you a lesson when we get home!"

He pulled the judge by the arm and led him down into the mosque. All who were in the mosque came out running when they saw how the farmer was beating the judge and said, "What are you doing? This is our judge! Release him!"

"Friends," replied the farmer, "I own this one-eyed donkey. I loaded him up with goods and told him to go to our business friend in Mosul. But he decided to go to Baghdad and has become a judge here; now you tell me what am I to do? He has cost me a great deal of time and trouble."

When the people realised that the intelligence of the farmer was very low and that he was really an idiot, they asked him the price of the donkey. The farmer replied: "The donkey together with his load was worth five hundred piasters". Hearing this they gave him this sum of money and told him to go back to his family.

THE DAUGHTER OF THE THORN-SELLER

Once upon a time, there ruled a Sultan in Baghdad. He died leaving a fifteen year old son as his heir. One day, the youth's mother came and said to him, "I wish that you get married so that I may rejoice in your happiness and see your children!" The prince, who had not yet set his eyes on a girl he fancied, was not willing to satisfy his mother's desire.

One day, while out hunting in the desert, the prince came to a stream. Being tired, the prince stopped for a drink. As he bent down to drink he saw a piece of paper lying beside the brook. It was a picture. He picked it up and gazed at it, but he was so moved by what he saw that he lost consciousness. After a while, he came back to his senses, and his slave said to him, "O master, what is it that has struck you like this?"

The prince said, "Let us go back to the palace for I do not feel like hunting today."

They returned to the palace, and the prince immediately went to see his mother. His mother was worried to see him back so soon, and was afraid something might be wrong.

The prince said to her, "My mother, do you still wish to see me married?"

She answered, "Of course! Nothing will make me happier."

He said, "Then I will only marry the girl in this picture!" and he showed her the piece of paper he had found lying beside the stream.

His mother said, "My son, how do you marry a stranger just like this. Why not marry one of your uncle's seven daughters?"

The prince was stubborn, "I am not interested in any of my ugly cousins. Either I marry this girl or none."

His mother was perplexed, but said, "I will do what I can."

The next day she went out with a slave, and began asking at the houses of Baghdad from door to door whether the original of the portrait lived there, and whether anyone knew her, but all to no avail! Nobody knew who the girl was.

After several days of enquiries, the mother finally said, "There is no girl in Baghdad to compare with the beauty of this portrait. I will go out into the desert and try my fortune there among the Bedouin!", and she fared forth into the desert.

In time she came across a maiden. After exchanging greetings the maiden asked her, "O my aunt, are you lost? Can I be of assistance to you?"

The prince's mother answered her, "I have come to search for the girl in this picture. My son has fallen in love with her and will marry none other! Can you assist in finding who is she?"

The girl said, "O my aunt, your quest is near its end. There in that house lives a thorn-seller with his three daughters. The eldest is the one in this portrait, the middle is even more beautiful. As for the third, she is so beautiful, that you will not believe your eyes when you see her!"

The prince's mother said, "Is that so? Take me there."

The maiden guided her to the door of the thorn-seller's house. The mother knocked at the door and was received by the thorn-seller's wife who welcomed her in.

Then the hostess called out to her eldest daughter to bring water for the guest. When the girl came in with a jug of water, the prince's mother looked at her and then at the picture, and sure enough it was the same girl.

Some time later the thorn-seller's wife called out to her second daughter, and asked her to bring some fruit. When the lady saw the second girl she observed that she was even lovelier than the first.

Then the woman called out to her youngest daughter, and told her to bring coffee. When the prince's mother saw the third daughter, she was amazed by her beauty, for she was more beautiful than her two elder sisters, and was the loveliest creature the lady had ever set eyes on!

After partaking of the refreshments, the prince's mother raised the subject of her son with the thorn-seller's wife, by saying, "I only have one son, and I would like to have him marry your daughter."

The thorn-seller's wife replied, "My three daughters are before you. Take whichever one of them you wish!"

The lady said, "I will take the youngest for my son. Do not bother yourself with presents or raiment, for I will provide her with all that she needs. She shall have all the jewels and the gold that she desires.

In some two weeks, after I have finished all the arrangements for the wedding, I will send for her." The thorn seller's wife said, "It shall be as you command!"

The prince's mother returned to the palace where her son was anxiously waiting for her.

He asked anxiously, "Did you find the owner of the picture?"

His mother cried triumphantly, "Indeed I have found her! I went out into the desert, and good fortune led me to the house of a thorn-seller, and the picture is that of his eldest daughter. His second daughter is even lovelier than she. And as for the youngest daughter, she is so lovely that I decided to choose her as your wife."

The next day the mother began preparing for the wedding. She ordered the wedding chamber to be decorated. From the jeweller she ordered jewels, and from the robe-maker dresses, and from the 'aba-maker, 'abas. In two weeks she sent for the bride, and invited guests for the ceremony.

When eventually she came to the house, all the guests were astonished by her beauty, for indeed, no lovelier bride had ever been seen.

In the meantime, the prince had gone to the bath with his slave. As he was returning, he had to pass beneath the windows of his seven ugly cousins. These cousins were envious that the prince was marrying somebody other than one of them. They were determined not to let the marriage take place. When they saw the prince coming, they began to talk as if they didn't know that he could hear them.

The eldest cousin said, "Did you see our cousin's bride?"

The second said, "Yes, and I have never seen such ugliness!"

The third said, "She is stooped!"

The fourth said, "She is blind!"

The fifth said, "She is black!"

The sixth said, "Her nose is crooked (*akcham*)!"

The seventh said, "She has yellow teeth!"

The prince heard what they were saying, and said to himself, "My cousins seem to have had a chance to see the bride. They could not be making this up as they do not know I would hear it. Could my mother have deceived me? It seems that my bride is not the beauty that she led me to expect, but as ugly as they have said!"

He decided not to proceed any further, and sent his slave to the palace to tell his mother that he would have nothing to do with the new bride. And he went to his country house outside Baghdad and did not come to the palace where his bride and all the guests were waiting for him.

The slave went to the palace and gave the prince's message to his mother. The prince's mother was upset at this sudden change of mind after all the preparations and expectations, and asked the slave, "What made him change his mind? Has he seen or talked to anybody?"

The slave replied that he had spoken with no one.

She did not know what to do. People were expecting to witness the wedding and the bride was ready in her chamber. Knowing her son's nature, and his obstinancy when angry, she decided to do nothing then. She informed the guests that her son would join them later, as something unexpected had come up. No one knew what had happened.

When all the guests had departed, she went to the bride and said to her, "My daughter, it seems that my son is angry with me, and when he is angry we do not ask him or talk to him. Maybe he will not come to you tonight! Maybe he will come tomorrow, if Allah wills." The girl took her clothes and went to bed.

The prince remained in his house for days and days, and the bride and her mother-in-law remained in the palace. Weeks and months passed, until three whole years passed. His mother never knew what had angered the prince, and why he had abandoned his lovely bride.

One day, it so happened that the son of the Sultan of a neighbouring kingdom was to be married. As was customary they invited the ladies in Baghdad's palace to the wedding. The prince's mother wished to go to the wedding, but her daughter-in-law could not go, for it is a shame for a bride to visit another bride. It also was perceived to bring bad luck. These were the customs and beliefs of Baghdad at that time.

So the woman said to her daughter-in-law, "My daughter, I am invited to a wedding, and so am obliged to leave you here alone in the palace. I shall be gone for seven days, and perhaps my going to this wedding will bring us good fortune and my son will come to you!"

The bride answered, "Go, my mother! Do not worry about me. I will manage on my own."

Now, the bride, even though she was a girl of the desert, was a clever girl. She had thought of an idea which she hoped would bring her husband back to her.

Now that her mother-in-law had gone, she decided to put her plan into action. So, the next day the girl called her servant, and asked him, "Can I trust you with a secret?"

The servant answered, "Indeed, my lady."

She said, "What I ask is this, go and get me a fine mare. I will enrich you for this and Allah will shower you with his benevolence."

He said, "Your wish, my lady, is my command. I will do it."

From the palace she chose a man's dress consisting of a rich *zboon*, an *'aba*, and an embroidered belt. When she put on these clothes, she looked as beautiful a boy as ever rode the streets of Baghdad. She got on the mare and rode out.

She rode around the city until eventually she came to her husband's house. She knocked at the garden gate, and the prince's gardener replied, "Who is it?"

The girl answered, in verse,

Ana khashab al azhar
I am flower-wood,
Kul men yushufni yisker
whoever sees me loses reason,
Shedda warid asfar
for a bouquet of yellow roses,
U be ghazi adhaab ahmar
I shall give a gold coin."

The gardener opened the gate, and, marvelling at the youth's beauty, started to gather a bunch of yellow roses which the youth asked of him. While he was doing so, the youth rode his mare amongst the flowers trampling them underfoot. Then he came back to the gardener, took the bouquet and gave him a handful of gold coins and rode off.
The prince looked out of the window of his room and saw how ruined the garden was. He called the gardener and angrily asked him what had happened to his garden.

The gardener answered, "O Prince! I do not know! I was not here! My son was sick and I went to him. When I got back the garden was the mess you see!" The prince commanded him to put the garden straight again.

The gardener set to work. He swept the paths, and put the flower beds in order. He trimmed the hedges where the mare had trampled them over. He watered the garden and did all he could to repair the damage.

The next day the girl dressed herself again in men's clothes and rode through the town until she came to her husband's house.

There she knocked at the garden gate, and the gardener cried, "Who is it?"

She answered,
"I am flower-wood,
whoever sees me loses reason,
for a bouquet of yellow roses,
I shall give a gold coin."

The gardener opened the door, then he went to pick her the flowers she asked for, while she, as before, rode her mare over the flower beds and hedges, striking them down with her stick. Then she went to the gardener, took the flowers, threw him a handful of gold coins and rode away.

When the prince looked out of the window, and saw the garden in a worse mess than it was the day before, he was furious and sent for his gardener.

The gardener presented himself, and the prince said to him, in angry tones, "Gardener, the garden is in a worse state than ever! Who shall you tell me is ill today? Your mother?"

The gardener answered, "O Sultan! I ask your mercy!"

He said, "Speak the truth!"

The gardener spoke, "For the past two days, a youth has been coming to this garden, whose beauty is the like of which I have never seen. He comes to the gate and says,

"I am flower-wood,
whoever sees me loses reason,
for a bouquet of yellow roses,
I shall give a gold coin,"

and when I open the gates for him, he rides his mare over the garden and leaves the mess you have seen."

The prince asked, "Why did you not tell me this yesterday?"

The gardener answered, "O Prince, I was afraid, and I thought he might not come back again."

The prince was intrigued. He said to the gardener, "If he comes tomorrow, bring him to see me. "

The gardener answered, "As your Highness commands!"

The third day came, and the girl did what she had done the previous two days. When she arrived at her husband's house and knocked at the gate, the gardener asked, "Who is it?" She answered with the same verse. He opened the gate and ran and told his master that the youth had come.

The prince came down to the garden, and when he saw the 'lad', amazement overcame him. He greeted him, and said, "You are my guest, you must come into my house. Welcome!" And led him to his *diwan*.

He served him sweets, and fruit, and juices and coffee, never taking his eyes off his beauty, and saying to him to come every day so that they might amuse themselves together.

The 'lad' replied, "Certainly I will come! And I ask your pardon for what I did to your garden!"

The prince said, "Do not worry about my garden. We all are at your feet, do with us what you want. Only visit us every day."

At last the 'lad' said, "My people will wonder where I am tarrying. I must return to them."

The prince said, "I hate to part with you so soon."

But the 'lad' insisted on leaving. Before he left, the prince invited him to come to his palace that night. And the 'lad' was glad to accept this invitation.

And the prince walked with him to the garden gate. As they were walking in the garden, the 'lad' pricked his finger on a rose bush. The prince tore off a piece of his embroidered shawl and wrapped it tenderly around the 'lad's' finger. The prince watched him till he was out of sight.

In the meantime, the prince's mother was at the neighbouring Sultan's wedding. She had told the women there of her troubles, and they had comforted her, saying, "Allah is so Merciful! He may open a new door with fortune after our wedding." The mother sighed and said, "My son is stubborn, but God works miracles!"

Back in his house, the prince called his slave, and commanded him to go to the palace and tell his mother that the prince was throwing a party at the palace that night. They must make all the necessary preparations.

The slave was delighted to hear such a change of mood and ran to the palace. When he got there, he knocked at the door and cried, "My lady, my master has sent me to say that there will be a feast tonight at his palace."

He was informed by his servants that the lady had not come back from the wedding in the neighbouring city. So he rushed there and relayed the message to the prince's mother.

A great joy entered the mother's heart. Her joy was immense, and her hosts said, "Did we not say that our wedding may bring you good fortune?"

She returned quickly to the palace, and sent for the cook and the servants and ordered them to prepare a magnificent feast.

Then she hurried to the bride, "Prepare yourself. Go to the bath, and put on your wedding dress, for your husband is coming."

When all was ready, the bride sat in the marriage chamber in all her finery. She was as lovely as ever.

After sundown, the prince came from his house, and waited impatiently for the 'lad'. While pacing the terrace, he passed the bridal chamber, where his bride was waiting.

As he was passing by the window, he heard a sound of moaning and at last he cried, "What is the matter? Are you in pain?"

His bride answered from within, "There was pain, but then he tore his shawl and wrapped it around my finger!"

The prince immediately recognised the voice and understood the words, and opened the door, crying, "By Allah, is it you?"

And when he looked at her, he was spellbound, and he fell at her feet, crying, "Was it you?"

She asked him beseechingly, "Why have you kept me imprisoned here all these years? What did I do to deserve this?"

He replied remorsefully, "What can I say? It was because of the evil tongues of my ugly cousins!"

The prince commanded that wedding festivities should extend for seven days and seven nights, and guests were entertained, and the dancers danced, and the drums beat, and the music played.

Then the bridegroom said to all present, "O all of you who love me, what shall I do to my seven evil cousins, who caused me and my lovely bride such misery these three years?"

The guests replied with one voice, "Cut off their heads ! "

But his bride, being of a nature as sweet as she was beautiful, restrained him and urged him to be merciful.

So the prince decided to banish the seven ugly and evil cousins from Baghdad forever.

THE PROPAGATING COOKING POTS

Once there lived in the city of Mosul a niggardly man, whose fist was always closed and who took extremely good care of everything that was his. He was well-known as the *bakheel*, the miser.

One day a neighbour decided to play a practical joke on the miser. But when he informed his friend of his intention, they asked, "How do you intend to do that ?"

"In good time you'll hear about it!" The joker said.

He went to the miser and said, "I am having a party with many guests and would like to borrow the biggest cooking pot you have."

The miser first hesitated for fear that something might happen to the pot and then informed his neighbour that he did not have the right pot for his use.

After the neighbour persisted in his request the miser relented and lent him a big pot.

The next day the neighbour brought the cooking pot back and put a smaller one inside it.

The miser asked, "What is this small pot doing here?

The neighbour replied, "I think that the big pot must have given birth to a small pot. It always happens with me that borrowed pots give birth to smaller ones."

The miser was so pleased to have gained a new pot that he never bothered to question the validity of that ludicrous statement about pots giving birth.

Few days later the neighbour approached the miser again and asked to borrow a pot which the miser lent without much hesitation. The joker used it and again put another small pot in it before he returned it to the miser.

"Another cooking pot!" Exclaimed the miser.

"I told you that that is what happens to me every time I borrow a cooking pot," replied the joker.

The miser was very pleased, because he was gaining one new pot every time he lent a big pot to his neighbour. This happened for the third time and the miser had gained three small cooking pots as a result of lending big pots to his neighbour.

Some time later the neighbour asked the miser to lend him five of his biggest cooking pots because he was having a very large party. Without any hesitation the miser lent him his best and biggest pots with the hope that he was soon to gain five new small pots.

But days passed and the neighbour had not returned the borrowed pots. The miser could not wait any longer. He went to his neighbour and asked, "Why have you not returned the pots yet?" The neighbour replied, "O my dear friend, I am so ashamed to face you."

"Why, what's the matter?" asked the miser.

"All the five big pots, which I borrowed from you, died while giving birth!" replied the joker.

"And how could that be. Have you ever heard of a pot dying ?" Asked the miser.

"Why not", replied the joker. "A pot that can give birth can equally die in childbirth. Every time I gave you a small pot you took it with delight and never questioned how pots could give birth. If your pots have died, there is very little I can do more than feel sorry for them."

The miser knew then that he had been the victim of a practical joke. He never told his story to anyone.

THE TAILOR'S DAUGHTER

Once upon a time, long ago, there was a Sultan who ruled the land of Iraq. This Sultan had among his attendants a tailor who was very good at making clothes. Modesty, however, was not one of this tailor's virtues, and he boasted of his talents and his famous customers to all and sundry.

Hearing that the tailor had been boasting of his skill, the Sultan sent for him. When he came into the royal presence, the Sultan told him that he had a job for him, and pointed to a stone lying outside in the garden saying, "Pick that stone up and bring it to me!"

The tailor did as he was commanded.

"Take the stone home with you," said the Sultan, "and show your skill by sewing me a stone coat!"

The tailor was afraid of the consequences of his imminent failure. He tried to explain to the Sultan that no man could make a coat out of stone. However, the Sultan displayed extreme anger and cried, "If within three days you do not deliver the stone coat I will have your head cut off!"

The tailor returned home convinced that the Sultan was bent on killing him and had only created an excuse to do so. He informed his family of the impending calamity because he could not see a way of making a coat out of a stone.

His wife and three daughters wept with him after hearing him telling them the story and lamenting his fate. However, his youngest daughter, the more thoughtful, said to her father, "There is no reason to despair, *Baba*. I think it is very easy to escape the Sultan's wrath."

"How is it easy, daughter, can't you see that in three days I am a dead man?" Replied her father.

The daughter instructed her father on what to do the next day.

The next morning the tailor asked to see the Sultan. When he was admitted, he showed his respect and placed a bag on the ground before him.

"What is this bag for?" asked the Sultan.

The tailor replied, "Your Majesty, I have designed and cut the stone ready to sew a fine garment for you. However, I have just realised that your Majesty has not supplied me with a suitable thread. So today, I have brought some sand in this bag and would like, your Majesty, to order that some thread be made from it so that I can finish my interesting work very soon."

The Sultan, realising that the game was over, laughed, and complimented the tailor for his trick. "I accept that you have saved your neck, but you could not have thought this out by yourself. Tell me who really figured it out for you," said the Sultan.

"How perceptive is your Majesty," said the tailor. "It was my youngest daughter who saved my head!" "How old is she?" asked the Sultan. "She is sixteen", said the tailor.

"At sixteen she is a wise girl, then I shall take her for a wife and she shall have a house of her own to live in", said the Sultan.

The tailor ran home to break the good news to his daughter and family. Marriage was completed soon afterwards and the young girl moved to her new house. However, when the time came for the bridegroom to join his bride, the Sultan did not appear. The bride waited for him day after day, but he never came.

It looked as though the Sultan had forgotten about her. The only time he would remember her was when he went out hunting. He would knock on her door and ask her, "O tailor's daughter, how are you?"

The bride responded that she was well. The tailor was anguished for his daughter's predicament, but he could do nothing.

One day the Sultan decided to go on a voyage to the land of Rum. As soon as she heard that her husband was going away, the tailor's daughter disguised herself and followed him until she came to his camp. There she pitched for herself a splendid tent. In the evening she walked out in the valley and reached the place where the Sultan had pitched his camp.

The Sultan's coffee-maker was making coffee at the fire when she passed by. When he saw her beauty, he was so distracted that, without knowing he put salt instead of sugar into the coffee.

When the Sultan tasted the coffee, he had the coffee-maker brought before him. The coffee-maker confessed to the Sultan that the reason for his distraction was that a girl as beautiful as the moon had passed by.

The Sultan was curious by this story and ordered that this beautiful girl be found. They reported to him that she was staying in a fine tent in the same valley where he was camping. The Sultan at once proceeded to visit her. He was well received and shown hospitality. He was so charmed by the young girl that he stayed three days and three nights with her.

On the third night they played chess, but the Sultan was so deeply infatuated that he thought of his opponent more than of the game, and lost to the lady. As a prize, he pulled from his finger a costly ring and placed it on hers. That dawn, while the Sultan was fast asleep, she hastily departed for home.

After her disappearance the Sultan could find no pleasure in his journey. He terminated his trip and went home. The tailor's daughter gave birth to a lovely boy whom she called Rum.

Some time later the Sultan decided a change would do his lonely heart some good and decided on another journey to Armenia. He went on his journey and reached the outskirts of a town and camped there. Again his abandoned wife followed him. The Sultan, who could not believe his luck, rushed to see her. Again they spent three nights in love and pleasure.

On the third night, as before, when he lost the game of chess, he gave her a jewelled dagger. Again she fled at dawn while he was still asleep and the heartbroken Sultan returned alone to his land. The tailor's daughter, in nine months, gave birth to a lovely boy she called Armenia.

Again the Sultan set on a new journey to reach Semerkend. Once more his wife followed him in disguise, and again he was overwhelmed with joy when he found her. Three days and nights passed, and the Sultan gave her his gold embroidered scarf when he lost the game of chess.

He was determined that night not to fall asleep, but she laced his drink with *benj* that put him into deep sleep. In due course she gave birth to a girl she called Semerkend.

Ten years passed during which the Sultan mourned the lady he had lost. At last he thought that in order to get over her he had to take a new wife. The daughter of a neighbouring Sultan was chosen and marriage was arranged. The people lined the streets to see the bride and her procession ride in to the city.

On the day of the wedding, the tailor's daughter put a plan into operation. She put the ring on the finger of Rum, the dagger into Armenia's belt and the scarf upon Semerkend's head. She then told her children to stand on the steps of the palace, and instructed them on what to do.

The three children did as their mother instructed them to do. When the Sultan's passed by, Rum cried to his brother, "Armenia, take care of our sister Semerkend, lest she gets run over."

This caught the Sultan's attention who thought a while about it. He called the three to him, and asked them for their names. He immediately recognised his three gifts, and ordered them to reveal how they came to have these gifts. Rum, the eldest, answered, "Mother was given them by our father every time she won a game of chess".

"Where is your mother?" Asked the Sultan.

He was taken by the three children to their mother. The Sultan discovered that the tailor's daughter, whom he had neglected for so many years, was the lady who stole his heart. He ordered that the new bride be sent back to her country.

The tailor's daughter moved to the palace and lived with her three children and the Sultan in joy and happiness.

TWO TALES OF HAROON AR RASHEED

I

The Khalifa Haroon ar Rasheed was walking in Baghdad, one day, accompanied by his chief minister.

They came to the bank of the Tigris, where they met a rug-cleaner cleaning rugs in the river. It was a bitterly cold winter day and so the Khalifa asked the man, "You have twelve, do you need these three?"

The rug-cleaner replied, "Yes, I need them for the thirty-two!"

The Khalifa asked, "And the far?"

"It is now near!" Replied the rug-cleaner.

The Khalifa finally said, "If I send you a goose will you pluck it?" To which the rug-cleaner replied, "Yes, I will surely pluck its feathers and return it to you!"

Then the Khalifa and his minister walked for a short distance when the Khalifa turned to his minister and asked, "Did you understand my questions to the rug-leaner?"

"O Commander of the faithful, how could I understand ?" Enquired the minister.

The Khalifa said, "I will give you three hours to find out the meaning of my conversation with the rug-cleaner. If, by then, you fail to explain to me what was said, you may lose your head."

The minister then hurriedly took leave of the Khalifa. He hurried to his house and took all the gold coins he had and returned to the rug-cleaner.

When he found the rug-cleaner, he said to him in anguish, "O may Allah protect you and your children. What was the meaning of what went on between you and the Khalifa."

The rug-cleaner replied, "It is none of your business. *Itmesha,* Move on!"

The minister pleaded with him saying, "My brother, if you will not tell me, I will lose my head! May Allah protect you! Have mercy on me! And explain to me the meaning of what went on between the Khalifa and you."

The rug-cleaner said, "Only if you give me a hundred pieces of gold for each riddle then will I speak." The minister gave him the first hundred pieces of gold.

The rug-cleaner began, "When the Khalifa asked me, 'You have twelve, do you need these three?', he meant that as there are twelve months in the year, do I really need to work during the three cold winter months. To which I replied, 'I need them for the thirty-two', by which I meant my teeth. For if a poor man remains idle three months, then he would not be able to eat!"

Then the minister said, "What of the second riddle?"

The rug-cleaner said firmly, "First the second hundred pieces of gold!" As the minister counted out the other hundred, the rug-cleaner continued, "'The far is now near' referred to my sight, which has grown longer with age."

"What about the goose?" Asked the excited minister.

The rug-cleaner replied, " When you give me all the gold that remains in the bag, I will explain the riddle about the goose."

The minister, reluctantly, handed him the bag, and the rug-cleaner said, "The Khalifa asked if he were to send me a goose, whether I would pluck it. By the goose he meant you, and, by Allah, I have plucked you!"

"Now you can go back to the Khalifa and explain these riddles. You have lost your gold to a poor man, but you have saved your neck!" The minister departed in shame.

II

One day the Khalifa, Haroon ar Rasheed, was walking in the streets of Baghdad with one of his companions.

Presently they came upon a man lying naked on the road. His body and limbs were painted in assorted colours.

The Khalifa poked him gently with his foot and said, "Have you no shame? Why are you sleeping naked?"

The man answered angrily, "Leave me alone!"

"And why have you painted yourself like this?" Asked the Khalifa

The man replied, "I intend to sleep. Suppose while asleep, someone came and cut off my limbs, and walked away with them, how should I recognise them again unless they were identified through paint?"

The Khalifa could not help bursting out into laughter, and said, "This man is 'msoaden, mad!" He then said to the man, "Get up and come to my palace. You can live in the kitchen; help the cook and earn your living."

Thus, the man was installed in the Khalifa's kitchen, and the Khalifa ordered that he should be treated well, fed well and given only light tasks such as peeling onions.

It happened that a neighbouring Sultan sent his Wazir to the Khalifa with the intention of testing him with a few riddles. When the Wazir entered into the Khalifa's presence, he said, "My master the Sultan sent you two riddles. If you can solve them, there will be peace between our two countries, but if you fail there will be war!"

"Speak!" the Khalifa commanded, and the Wazir told him the riddles.

But the Khalifa did not understand the riddles. The 'msoaden noticed that something was troubling the palace and enquired what it was. They answered him, "Why would a madman like you be interested in these matters?"

But the 'msoaden replied indignantly, "I may be mad, but even mad people can sometimes help."

He kept on asking until they went to the Khalifa and said to him, "The madman in the kitchen thinks that he can help you solve the riddles!"

The Khalifa said, "Why not. Let him come! Perhaps a stone can help when wise men fail".

They brought the madman in, and everybody in the palace was anxious to witness what was happening. The visiting Wazir repeated the riddles to the madman:

He drew a circle on the ground with his finger. The madman drew a line across the circle. Then the Wazir took from his pocket an egg and placed it in the centre of the circle. The madman took out an onion from his pocket and placed it next to the egg.

Then the Wazir asked him to explain the meaning.

The madman said, "Your circle was the world, and my line cutting across it symbolises the two spheres. The egg, with its yolk and white, represents the waters of the earth and the sun which give it life; the onion, with its seven skins, symbolises the seven layers of the earth."

The Wazir said in amazement, "No madman could have solved these riddles. It must have been Allah who inspired him to speak "

Everybody applauded. The Wazir departed satisfied and war was averted.

THE MAGIC LAMP

In Baghdad in an age long ago, there lived a merchant who had been married for many years, but was not blessed with a child. This was a cause of great sorrow to him and his wife. On one sunny spring day, while sitting in his shop in the *suq as Safafiir*, three *daraweesh* came and spoke to him.

They enquired about the cause of his great sorrow, and they then gave him an apple and instructed him to peel it and cut it in half. Half the apple he was to eat himself, and the other half he was to give to his wife to eat. The peel was to be given to the mare. After this, *Inshallah*, their prayers would be answered. The *daraweesh* promised the old merchant that Allah would give them a boy who, when fully grown, would find a great treasure hidden under ground.

The merchant did as he was instructed. The merchant's wife, despite her advanced age, became pregnant, and after nine months, bore a boy, a beautiful child. The father praised and thanked Allah for his mercy, and rewarded the *daraweesh* bountifully. The mare also brought forth a foal!

Years passed, and the boy grew up. He was the apple of his mother's eye, and he was so beautiful that his parents did not allow him to leave their sight; he had to remain inside their *hosh* .The old merchant died when the boy was fifteen, and since he used to provide the income, after his death, the family became very poor.

131

The boy had always wished to go outside the *hosh*, and he would often ask his mother, "*Mama, aku naas mithli*? Are there humans like me? "And his mother would reply, "Yes, there are boys like you in the world."

However, whenever he sought permission to go outside, she refused, even after his father's death. The boy would insist, "We are now so poor, and we barely have enough money to buy food. We cannot live like this; I must go out and work to earn us some money." The mother still refused, and said, "We are not going to disregard your father's wishes just because he is dead."

However one day the boy found the *Bab-il-hosh*, the main door, unlocked, and he sneaked out. Being the intelligent boy that he was, he made sure to remember where his house was. As he was walking he saw a *beshlik* (a coin from the Ottoman period) on the ground, he picked it up and used it to buy some bread and meat. He then hurried home, returning along the same way he had come. When his mother saw the food, she was surprised, and enquired, "Where did you get this food from, my son?" He answered, "It is from Allah."

When the food ran out, the boy ventured out again, and this time he dared to go further from home. Again he found a *beshlik* and bought food with it. When his mother asked him about the food, he replied, "It is from Allah".

This continued until one day he decided to go to the *suq*. He walked to the *suq*, and there he was fascinated by the fine shops, and the vibrancy of the merchants and shoppers. He, being a handsome young man, was himself admired by all those who saw him

It so happened that the eldest of the three *daraweesh* was in the *suq*.

As soon as he saw the boy, he recognised him; went to him and kissed him on both cheeks, saying, "My son! How are you? You are the son of my brother and I shall be like a father to you. I am so happy to see you!"

The *darweesh* gave the boy a gold coin and asked him to take him to his house. The boy brought the *darweesh* to his house, and ran up and asked his mother excitedly, "O mother, did you know that my father had a brother?" She said bewilderedly, "No... I never knew that he had a brother."

The boy continued, "There is a man below who says he is my father's brother, and he has given me this piece of gold."

They welcomed the *darweesh* into their home, and he later moved to live with them. He often gave the boy money to buy merchandise, and soon the boy was able to start a business, trading in silk, and other fine items. The business, in a short period of time, prospered and their wealth increased.

Many years passed, then one day the *darweesh* suggested that the boy go with him to hunt in the desert. They travelled deep into the desert, and then suddenly the *darweesh* paused and said, "Below my feet is a great treasure. On my command, a passage will appear in the ground, and you must go down this passage. Deep inside you will find a garden, the like of which you have never seen. You will see emeralds, rubies, and diamonds growing on trees, but you must not pick them! If you begin to pick them, the passage will close on you for ever!"

The *darweesh* continued, "In the middle of the garden you will find an oil lamp, which you should bring back and give to me. However, in case you get into any trouble, take this ring with you and rub it when you need help." The *darweesh* then sat down in front of a fire and started to read his spells, until finally the earth split open revealing a passage, with stairs leading deep into the ground.

The boy descended carefully down the stairs, and soon found himself in an enchanting garden abound with crystals, emeralds, and diamonds. However, the boy could not resist temptation, and despite the clear warning he had received, he filled his pockets with all kinds of jewels.

He then sighted the lamp, which he picked up and slipped into his shirt, but then the surroundings became very dark. The earth had closed and trapped him inside. Above ground, the *darweesh* waited for seven whole days, but there was no sign of the boy.

He realised that the boy must have become greedy. In the meantime, at the boy's house in Baghdad it was assumed that the boy had been killed by the *darweesh* or had just got lost and died. His mother began an '*aza*, a session where women wail in mourning.

Underground, the boy never gave up searching for a way out, but it was not until the seventh day, when he accidentally rubbed his ring on a rock, that the earth opened. He climbed up the steps and he saw the *darweesh* waiting for him at the top. The boy told the *darweesh* the whole story and emptied his pockets of all the jewels at the *darweesh's* feet.

The *darweesh* was not interested, all he enquired about was, "Where is the lamp I asked you to bring back for me?"

The boy thought to himself, "Why does he value the oil lamp so much more than these jewels. The lamp must be very precious." Thus the boy said to the *darweesh*, "I did not see any lamp." When the *darweesh* heard this, he uttered a sharp scream, fell back, and died.

The boy, rather perplexed, went back to Baghdad with the jewels and the lamp. He brought great joy to his mother and she turned her mourning and wailing into rejoicing. After the boy sold the exquisite jewels, he became one of the richest merchants in the town.

Some months later, while the mother was cleaning the house, she found the lamp, and said to herself, "How dirty this oil lamp is. I must clean it." She began to clean it with a cloth, and as she started to rub it, the room was suddenly filled by smoke emanating from the oil lamp, and she saw seven *jinn* standing with their arms folded. The largest of them spoke to her:

Labbeik, labbeik	"Your will, your will!
Ana 'abd bein edeek	I am your slave
Utlub we temenna	Ask and wish!"

The mother was terrified and ran to her son. After hearing the story, the boy came into the room and rubbed the lamp. He experienced what his mother had described. The boy was not as frightened, but asked for a magnificent crown; one with jewels, of every kind, embedded in it. The *jinn* said, "Close your eyes, and then open them!" The boy closed his eyes, and when he opened them he saw a magnificent crown upon a tray.

The boy then returned to his mother, and said, "Mother, take this tray and present it to the Sultan. If asked, tell him it is a gift from me." The mother did as her son wished. The Sultan looked at the crown, the like of which he had never seen before, and wondered why it was sent to him. He consulted his Wazir, and the Wazir thought it was a request for the Sultan's daughter's hand.

The Sultan then declared, "You may tell your son that I accept his gift and that I am willing to wed my daughter to him." The mother rushed home to give her son the good news, and the young man was so happy that he spent his time in merrymaking and amusement. He thought that since the Sultan had consented to give him his daughter, there was no hurry.

Over a year passed and the merchant's son had made no effort to claim his bride. A prince, from a neighbouring area, then asked for the Sultan's daughter's hand, and he was accepted as a future son-in-law.

However, when news reached the merchant's son that on the following day the Sultan's daughter was to be married, he became very angry and reproached himself for his indifference. He rubbed the lamp and when the seven *jinn* appeared, he explained his predicament and asked for help. The largest of the seven said, "It matters not. You need not trouble yourself; the princess is yours."

On the wedding night the prince entered his bride's room, but as soon as he looked at his bride, he fell to the floor like a log. He then spent the whole night on the floor, in that state. This went on for several nights. When the princess was then asked about her marriage, she answered, "There was no marriage! The groom sleeps like a log every night."

A few weeks later the merchant's son went to the Sultan and told him, "You promised your daughter to me, and yet you have given her to another man! I appeal to your honour."

The Sultan remembered his promise and bit on his finger saying, "I completely forgot. However, this is no bridegroom and so I shall dismiss him. She will then be yours."

The merchant's son married the Sultan's daughter, and the *jinn* of the oil lamp built him a fabulous palace next to that of the Sultan.

In the meantime, the two other *darweesh* had become very anxious about the disappearance of their eldest brother. They travelled from place to place, searching for their brother, until they finally came to the conclusion that he must have been killed by the merchant's son. The *daraweesh* decided to avenge the death of their brother, and so they went to Baghdad to find the merchant's son.

On arrival in Baghdad, they saw a fine palace adjacent to the Sultan's palace, and they knew that such beauty had to be the handicraft of *jinn*. They then concluded that this had to be the merchant's son's home, who had the palace built there in order to be close to his father-in-law.

After devising a plan, one of the *darweesh* went into the *suq*, and bought a basket and many beautiful oil lamps; he collected the most beautiful that he could find. He then walked along the streets in the manner of Baghdadi street vendors: the basket on his head and every few steps yelling, "I have fine lamps!...Fine lamps!"

Eventually, he came to the palace and the merchant's son's wife heard the *darweesh* hawking his lamps. She called a servant and told her to, "Call *Abul lampat*, the seller-of-lamps, so that I may see the lamps."

The *darweesh* displayed his basket, and began to look around the room, searching for the magic lamp. The princess looked at his wares, and chose one of them.

The *darweesh* said, "Take it. Take them all if you want. But in return give me the old and dirty one hanging on the wall!" He pointed to the magic lamp. The princess, thinking that the *Abul lampat* was crazy, laughed and said, "You may take it!"

The *darweesh* ran out, as fast as he could, with the lamp under his arm. The mother then came in, and was puzzled to find so many new lamps on the floor; the princess told her that the *Abul lampat* had given them to her in return for the old lamp. When the mother heard this, she screamed, "How could you have done that! That lamp made my son what he is toady!" The girl was terrified and said, "How should I have known? Nobody told me."

The *darweesh* left the city; rubbed the lamp and commanded the *jinn* to transfer the palace to his territory. When the merchant's son returned from his favourite sport of hunting, he saw his palace had disappeared; his mother hurried to him and told him what had happened.

The Sultan became very angry when he heard that his daughter had been taken. He summoned the merchant's son, and asked, "Where is my daughter?" The merchant's son told the whole story to the Sultan, and when he finished he said, "I am now going to look for my wife, and if I have not returned within thirty days, you should assume that I am dead."

He walked into the desert, and carried on walking for days. He finally came to an oasis where he was able to drink and wash his face. Fortunately, as he was washing his face he accidentally rubbed his magic ring, and as a result two black slaves appeared before him.

He said to them, "Fly me to the palace of the three *darweesh*. Do you know where their land is?" The black slaves answered, "We shall take you there, but do not ask us for anything more difficult; we are afraid of the seven *jinn* of the lamp," They then told him to, "Close and open your eyes". He found himself on the roof of the second *darweesh's* house.

At that time of day the *darweesh* was not in his house, and the princess was alone. The *darweesh* would have forced the princess to marry him immediately, had she not promised to marry him after the days of *'edda* were over.

The merchant's son climbed down from the roof, and went to the door of his wife's room. He knocked at the door gently. She asked, "Who is it?" All he said was, "I", but she immediately recognised his voice, and opened the door for him. They embraced each other and he asked her, "Where is our lamp?" She replied, "The *darweesh* carries it with him at all times; he wears it around his waist."

The merchant's son devised a plan, "I shall hide behind the door. When the *darweesh* comes back, remove your veil and tell him that you will marry tonight. But say to him that he must first drink with you; we shall prepare him a drink mixed with *benj*, anaesthetic."

She acted in accordance with the plan. As they drank, she gave him a cup of drink with *benj* in it. Not long afterwards the *darweesh* fell to the ground, and the merchant's son pounced on him and stabbed him to death.

The couple then took the lamp from the *darweesh* and rubbed it. In the blink of an eye, they and all their belongings were transported back to Baghdad.

Once back in Baghdad, the merchant's son rubbed the lamp again and asked the seven *jinn*, "Do I still have enemies?" They answered, "Yes, you still have one enemy left, and he will try to kill you, in two days time."

The third *darweesh*, the youngest of the three, knew that his brothers were killed by the merchant's son. He then went to Baghdad, and stood outside the merchant's son's palace plotting his revenge. He asked passers-by, "Does the princess ever leave the palace?" They informed him that she never leaves the house, but that, "There is a *maseyreh* , a nun, who visits her every Sunday."

As it was Sunday, the *darweesh* decided to wait. He stood in the shade and when he finally saw the *maseyreh*, he attacked and killed her. The *darweesh* then put on the *maseyreh's* clothes, and knocked on the palace door. "Who is it?" He replied, "I, the *maseyreh*."

The door was opened, and the *darweesh* thus entered the palace. The Sultan's daughter greatly appreciated the company of the *maseyreh*, and so she quickly came down the stairs into the courtyard. However, before she could reach the false *maseyreh*, her husband lunged from behind the door, and with one blow from his sharp sword, severed the *darweesh's* head sending it flying away.

The princess began to cry and wail, "Why have you killed the *maseyreh*? Have you gone mad?" The merchant's son showed her that the one he had killed was not the *maseyreh*, but it was the *darweesh* they had been expecting.

They then rejoiced at having outwitted the *darweesh*. The young man and his princess lived happily together and the lamp was kept in a special place in the palace from that day onwards.

A STORY OF SHAMSHUM AJ-JABBAR

There lived once in southern Iraq a very strong man called Shamshum aj-Jabbar, Shamshum the Mighty One. He was so strong that he could lift two camels with one arm and kill seven men with one blow!

Shamshum was married to a very beautiful daughter of a merchant. He loved her greatly, and in time she bore him a son.

But although Shamshum loved his wife dearly, she was unfaithful to him. She had some forty *deyus* for lovers. They used to visit her every day, after Shamshum went to work; they took her to their house in the desert, where she entertained them.

When the son grew up, he could not put up with his mother's behaviour and eventually told his father what the mother was doing and how ashamed he felt.

Shamshum decided to follow his wife accompanied by the *deyus* to their house. He then stormed into the house of the *deyus*; attacked them and dragged his wife back home.

But the wife was unrepentant. She kept on going with the *deyus* and every day he followed her and beat the *deyus* and brought her back. The *deyus* were amazed at his strength and ability to beat them up every day the way he was doing. They had to find out the secret of his strength in order for them to subdue him.

At last, frustrated, the *deyus* asked the woman to enquire from her husband the source of his strength. That night, in bed, she asked her husband " You are so strong! Where do you get your strength from?" Shamshum was unsure about the reason for that question and asked her, "Why do you want to know?

She replied, "Just out of interest."

Shamshum tried to be devious and said, "My strength derives from the flight of birds. As long as birds fly in the firmament, I am strong!"

On hearing this revelation, the *deyus* decided to catch and kill all the birds. After they were done, there were no birds left in the world. However, that did not solve their predicament. Shamshum carried on beating the *deyus* every day.

The *deyus* said to Shamshum's wife, "He lied to you! His strength is not in the birds! He continues to beat and batter us. Find out the source of his strength." That night she pressed him again to tell her from whence he gained his strength.

Shamshum, who had not figured out the game, answered, "My strength is in my broom. As long as brooms of wood are used and made, I am strong!" The next day the *deyus* collected all the brooms in the world and burned them. But again that was of no use as Shamshum carried on beating them every day.

The *deyus* requested his wife to try again and find out the source of his strength. At night she said to her husband, "I don' believe any of what you have told me. Why don't you tell me the truth about the source of your strength?"

Shamshum thought to himself, "What can a woman do to me to hurt me if I were to tell her the truth?" He said, "My strength is in my hair! As long as my hair is long, I am strong!"

The next day, she met the *deyus* and joined them in their house. There she told them that Shamshum's strength was in his hair. The *deyus* then instructed her to cut off Shamshum's hair while he slept.

That night, as Shamshum slept, his wife took a pair of shears and cut off his hair. When he woke up in the morning he was so weak that he could not even walk.

When the *deyus* arrived, they seized Shamshum the Mighty, and bound him with chains. They took him to the desert where they put him into a sack up to his armpits; dug a hole, and put him into it up to his chest. In order to hold him down they put a large slab of marble on his chest. There they left him to suffer before he died in revenge for the suffering he had caused them.

Shamshum did not die as very day his son came to him and gave him food and water. There Shamshum stayed for forty days. Each day his hair grew, and as his hair grew, his strength was being restored. On the fortieth day he said to his son, "Help me my son. With our combined strengths and the will of Allah we shall he able to throw this stone off my chest." The good son agreed eagerly.

They pushed and struggled, and made a great effort, until at last they pushed the great stone from Shamshum's chest, and threw it aside.

Shamshum then said, "My son, go home and bring me my sharp sword hanging on the wall. Be careful when you handle it." The boy went home; took down the sword from the wall and carefully carried it to his father.

Shamshum instructed his son on how to open the sack, and broke the chains which bound him. When that was done he said to his son, "Now, I will go and kill that *si'luwa,* your mother."

He reached the *deyu's* house and knocked at the door. As each *deyu* came out, he cut his head off. Thirty nine *deyus* came out and lost their heads before his wife stepped out and had her head cut off. But the fortieth *deyu* had two heads, and when Shamshum had cut one of his heads off, the *deyu* escaped with the other still on his shoulders.

Shamshum and his son wandered in the land, until eventually they came to a sea beyond which there was an island. On the seashore they saw a big serpent, coiled around the trunk of a tree. This serpent lived upon the nestling of an eagle which had its nest in the tree. Shamshum, on seeing the serpent, took his sword and killed it.

When the mother eagle flew back to her nest, and saw Shamshum and his son nearby, she was much angered. She said, "Son of Adam, is it you who comes each year and kills my brood? You shall surely die a terrible death!"

But the eaglets cried, "No! Mother, No! Mother, this Son of Adam did us no harm, but he saved us from the serpent which you now see dead!"

When the eagle saw the dead serpent, she was happy and grateful and said, "Son of Adam, you have saved my children from death. I will repay you with whatever you desire and wish."

Shamshum answered, "I only have one desire. Take me and my son to that distant island."

The eagle answered, "It shall be as you wish!" She spread her two wings, saying, "You get on one wing, and your son on the other." She flew them over the sea, and set them down on the island.

Shamshum wanted to live with his son in peace on that island. Shamshum, who was also wise and learned, taught his son all the knowledge he had.

But their island was a barren one and there was little to eat and drink. Subsequently Shamshum's son fell ill and died. Shamshum was much grieved, as he loved his son dearly. But what could he do! It was fate, the will of Allah.

Shamshum dug a hole in the earth, and made a tomb for his son and buried him. He then sat down beside the tomb and read and stayed reading and contemplating for many years.

He said to himself, "One day, I shall lie here beside my son. But I wonder who will bury me." He was so downhearted.

We return now to the *deyu* who had escaped with his life when Shamshum slew his brothers. This *deyu* of two heads was the lover of the Khalifa's daughter.

When he told her how Shamshum the Mighty cut off one of his heads she wanted to see him, and said, "Where is Shamshum the Mighty now?"

The *deyu* replied, "I do not know where he is now."

So the princess sent for sorcerers and witches and asked them to locate Shamshum for her. They made spells and answered her, "He is to be found, but he is very far."

At last the princess said to one of the skilled witches, "I want Shamshum, and if you find him, you shall have everything you want."

The skilled witch read in the sand and said, "I can see him in an island behind the sea." The princess said, "Take me to him, as I wish so much to see him."

The witch said, "There is no problem to transfer you to the island." She summoned some of her *jinn* and ordered them to transfer the princess to the island saying, "Take this *deywa* and drop her on the island which is in the sea beyond the seven seas".

The *jinn* flew her to the island as commanded.

While she was hovering over the island, the Khalifa's daughter saw Shamshum, who was by now an old man, reading from an open book upon the tomb of his son. When she had landed on the island, Shamshum lifted his eyes and saw her sitting upon the other side of the tomb and he asked her, "Are you human or of the *jinn*?"

"I am human." She said.

He asked, "What brought you here?"

She said, "I want to know all that has happened to you".

Puzzled, he said, "Why are you interested in my story?"

She answered, "I wish to know how you came to be here as I, too, have fallen into this island."

He nodded, "I will tell you my story, but on one condition. When you have listened to my story, you will kill me and bury me beside my son."

She agreed, "It shall be as you wish."

When he had finished telling his story, he said to her, "Now that I have told you my tale, you fulfill you part and cut off my head with my sword."

She cried, "That cannot be right. How can I cut off your head? I cannot do that!"

But he pleaded and pleaded with her telling her how miserable and lonely he was. He put the sword into her hand and begged her again. She then took the sword and cut off his head.

She dug him a grave beside his son's, and buried him.

And thus ends the story of Shamshum aj-Jabbar.

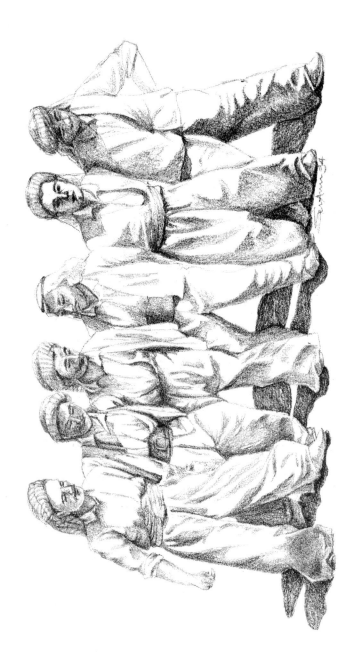

KURDISH TALES

I

One day, three Kurds were walking along the road in the mountains when they spotted a spring. As it was a hot summer's day, they said to one another, "Let us sit down here and rest, for it is a cool and beautiful spring."

They sat down and let their legs dangle in the water.

After a little while one of them shouted in a panic to the others, "Help me! I have lost my legs!"

His companions looked down into the water and also started to panic, "We have lost our legs too!"

One of them, a village elder, thought about it and suddenly had the bright idea that they should stay there until a caravan passed by and they could then call out to the people to help them retrieve their legs.

Around teatime the Sultan's caravan came along, and the Kurds called out, "For God's sake please come along and help us find our legs".

149

When the Sultan heard this, he dismounted from his steed and walked towards the three calling out, "Hey there, what is the matter with you?"

"We ask for your protection", they called out, "We came here and hung our legs in the pond. Now they are lost, and we beg you to help us get them back."

The Sultan was carrying a stick in his hand; this he raised and beat down on each Kurd two or three times. They jumped up in a great hurry and called out, "God bless your mother and father; our legs were lost, and you have helped us retrieve them."

The Sultan told his fellow travellers, "Take these people with you. I want to find out if they really are as stupid as they seem, or if they are planning mischief."

The Sultan ordered a sack of black raisins and a sack of beetles to be brought and emptied in front of the Kurds. He ordered the Kurds to eat what was emptied in front of them.

Seeing that the beetles were running off, one of them told the other, "Take those that are running away first! The others will be safe for later."

They began running after the beetles, and killed and ate them.

When the Sultan saw just how witless these people were, he gave each of them a thousand dinars and told them to go to their families.

II

One day, a Kurd told his wife to fetch some flour from a leather sack in the storeroom of their house. The sack was resting against a column in this room.

The wife went to the room to fetch flour and put a hand from one side of the column, and a hand from the other side of the column into the sack and picked up a handful of flour. When she tried to pull her hands out, she found she could not separate them. She tried for a long time without success.

Finally she called out, "For God's sake, come here! I cannot get my hands apart!"

Her husband and his friends came into the storeroom and saw the predicament, "We have to call the village council," they said. This was done.

After the village elders had studied the situation, they said, "There is no other solution but to ask ten men to come here - we will then stand their feet on supports so they can lift the ceiling with their backs. Then we can move the column and the woman will be able to release her hands."

The husband called ten men from the village who, when they arrived, were placed onto supports and they lifted up the ceiling with their backs. However, in doing this, the roof fell on top of them and killed them all.

III

Once upon a time there was a Kurd who owned an ox. One day, being thirsty, the animal put its head into a water jar that was in the house, and started to drink. When it tried to get its head out again, it could not, it was stuck in the jar.

The owner of the ox came home, and, alarmed at what he saw, called the village elders to his house to find a way of releasing the ox's head.

When they had all studied the predicament, they tried to find a solution. Finally they said, "There is no other way than to cut off the ox's head!"

Thus they fetched a knife and killed the ox. Having done this, the head fell into the bottom of the jar.

Once again, the question was what to do. After further deliberation, the village elders decided the jar had to be broken in order to release the head. The jar was broken and the ox's head was released, and thus the Kurd lost both his ox and his jar.

IV

In a village in the mountains of Northern Iraq, a group of Kurdish villagers were sitting together, talking amongst themselves, and saying, "We really cannot wait any longer. We must find out how deep our little valley really is. Someone might come along one day and ask us about it, then what shall we answer?"

The village elders, after some pondering, thought of a solution, saying, "We know how to go about it. We shall test how many men it takes to reach the bottom of the valley. One man will have to get a firm grasp, with both hands, around the peak of the hill, and let his legs dangle; then a second will descend and hold onto his feet, and so on, until they have reached the ground below. Then we shall know how many men deep the valley is."

They all agreed this idea was a good one and set off. One managed to get a firm hold on the peak with both his hands; a second climbed down and held onto his feet; then it became three to be suspended thus.

The first one, however, found that his arms were beginning to get tired and he called out to the others, "Wait, let me rest for a while!"

Saying this, he let go and they all fell to their death. Witnessing this, the village elders said to one another, "It does not really matter whether we know the depth of the valley or not."

THE DOVE AND THE FISHERMAN'S SON

One day, the Sultan ordered his town crier to announce to all people that no fires or lights were to be lit that night because he, the Sultan, intended to walk through the streets of Baghdad unnoticed.

When night fell, the Sultan and his Wazir set out on their stroll through the city's streets and alleys.

After a while, the Sultan and his companion saw a light in the distance. The Sultan asked, "Whose house can that be, to ignore our commands?"

They approached the source of the light, and saw that it came from a second-floor window of a house. The Sultan ordered the Wazir to climb up to see what was going on in that room.

Up climbed the Wazir, and when he got to the window, he looked in and saw three girls in the room. The girls were talking, and the Wazir cocked his ears to listen to what was being said.

The eldest girl was talking, and said, "If only Allah would make the Sultan's heart love me, and ask for my hand in marriage, I would make him a carpet so big that it would cover all his kingdom."

The second girl retorted, "If I were to marry the Sultan, I would make him a tent that would cover all his subjects".

Whereupon the youngest girl said, "If I were to marry the Sultan, I would bear him a son with locks of silver and gold."

The Wazir, having heard all that was said, climbed down from his perch and repeated what he heard to the Sultan, who was waiting below.

"Mark this house," the Sultan commanded, "so that we may find it again tomorrow." And it was done.

The next day, the Sultan ordered his Wazir to go to the house in question, and to ask for the hand of the eldest girl in marriage on his behalf. The Wazir did as he was ordered, and the marriage was agreed upon. There was great rejoicing when the wedding took place, and the bride was taken in procession to her husband's palace.

A few days later, the Sultan asked his new wife, "Where is the carpet you promise to make for me."

The girl replied, "The carpet is Allah's earth on which we stand." The Sultan punished her by making her a kitchen-maid.

The next morning, the sultan commanded the Wazir to go to the same house and ask for the hand of the second girl on his master's behalf.

The marriage was agreed upon, and the wedding took place, and the bride was taken amid celebration to her husband's palace.

After a few days passed, the Sultan asked his new bride, "Where is tent that you promised to make for me?"

The second bride replied, "The tent is the sky above us." He made her a kitchen-maid too.

So, as before, the next morning the Sultan commanded his Wazir to go forth and arrange his marriage to the youngest girl.

This was done amid much celebration.

After the passing of a few days, the king asked his new bride, "What about the son you promised me?"

The youngest bride replied, "I have prayed to Allah for a son. He can give him to me after the passing of nine months."

The days passed, and eventually, after nine months, the youngest bride gave birth to a son.

When the other two brides heard of this, they became jealous and angry. They pondered what to do, and decided to pay the mid-wife attending the youngest bride to take the boy and replace him with two black dogs. They paid her one thousand Dinars for doing this.

"You must tell the king that his wife give birth to two black dogs. The boy, however, you will bring to us!"

This was done; she gave the little boy to the sisters and then went before the Sultan. When he asked her for news of the birth, she answered him that his wife had given birth to two black dogs.

The Sultan was enraged when he heard this. He immediately ordered that the youngest bride should be taken outside the city walls, wrapped in camel skin, and given only a loaf of bread a day to eat. From that day on, all who passed to and from the city spat in her face and threw stones at her.

Meanwhile, the two scheming brides placed the boy in a basket and cast him in the Tigris.

The waves carried the basket down river until eventually a fisherman, plying his trade, spotted it and dragged it ashore.

The fisherman, who although married for many years had no child of his own, opened the basket, and was amazed at its contents.

He cried out to his wife, "O wife, Allah has not granted that you bear a child, but from the river He has given us a son!"

They were both overjoyed by Allah's gift, and started preparing for the boy's stay with them.

However, when the wife was bathing the baby in a tub, she was amazed to see that the water in the tub turned to gold!

The fisherman and his wife thus became rich and they raised the boy with love and kindness.

One day, when the boy had grown older and was playing with his friends, they started to taunt him saying that he was not the fisherman's son.

Saddened, he went to his father and asked, "Is it true that I am not your son?"
The fisherman replied, "No, you are not. I found you on the river when you were but a baby!"

The boy was extremely distressed when he heard this. A few days later, he went to his father and mother and declared that he would go out into the world to look for his real parents.

He rode out on a mare, and roamed the land until presently he reached a house. Being tired after his long ride, he entered it. Inside, he found a couch prepared, tea on the fire, and a water-pipe already lit.

The boy drank some tea, smoked the pipe, and then went to sleep on the couch. As he slept, a white dove alighted on the roof of the house. Seeing the boy sleeping inside, the dove changed into a beautiful girl, and entered the house and woke the young man from his sleep.

She asked him, "What has brought you here, for you look like a stranger." "Allah has sent me!" he replied.

She then asked him, "Will you take me as your wife, according to the ways of Allah and his Prophet?"

"Yes," he said, "but I cannot marry you until I have found my home."

So the girl said, "If you swear before Allah that you will take me as your wife, I will travel with you."

Whereupon the boy declared, "Yes, I swear it. I will take you as my wife. Come with me!"

The girl made him promise to do whatever she asked during their journey, and he agreed.

They set out on the road, and presently arrived at the city where his real father, the Sultan, ruled. They did not enter the city, but stayed in a grove of trees just outside. When they had dismounted, the girl said to the young man, "The Sultan takes a stroll in these gardens every day. When he sees you, and asks you to visit him, do not go!"

Presently, the Sultan, on his daily stroll, saw the youth, and he immediately liked him and desired to have him near him.

The youth went back to the girl and told her that the Sultan had invited him to visit the palace, but that he, the youth, declined the invitation.

She then instructed him, "When the Sultan sees you tomorrow, go to him and drink a cup of coffee with him, but leave without further delay."

Meanwhile, the Sultan returned to his palace, deep in thought. There he related to his wives that he had met a youth outside, whose locks were one of silver and one of gold.

The wives were worried and full of apprehension that this might be the child they threw in the river. They sent an old woman to the house where the strangers stayed to find out more about him. When the old woman arrived at the house, and tried to enter, the girl killed her.

On the following morning, the Sultan started for the orchard as soon as he had risen.

The girl had instructed the youth thus, "Today the king will invite you to his palace. You must go with him, but take this cat with you.

You must also take this bunch of flowers. When you get to the city gates, you will see a woman wrapped in a camel skin. Then go and see the Sultan. If, at the Sultan's palace, you are offered food, give some of it to the cat first. If it dies, do not touch the food. When the time comes for you to take your leave, the Sultan will offer you a mare. You are not to accept this gift, but tell him that if he wants to give you a favour, he should give you the woman that sits at the city gate."

The Sultan met the youth, and invited him to his palace. When they arrived there, they sat down and started to chat and drink coffee.

Later, when breakfast was served, the youth gave some of the food to the cat before he ate anything himself. No sooner had the cat tasted the food, than it dropped down dead.

"*Afarim*! Bravo, Sultan!", the youth exclaimed, "Is this the way you treat your guests?"

The Sultan was deeply embarrassed and ashamed, and when the youth discontentedly wanted to take his leave, the Sultan ordered for a mare to be brought for him as a gift.

"No, I do not want a mare," said the young man, "but if you want to give me a present, give me the woman in the camel-skin wrap who sits at the city gate."

"No!" the king replied, "I cannot give you this woman, for she has committed a vile deed, and must be punished!"

"As you please," said the youth, "but I do not want anything other than this woman," and made to leave.

When the king saw that the youth was going to leave, he retracted, saying, "All right, take the woman!"

The youth took the woman with him to where he and the girl were staying. As soon as the girl saw the woman, she came out and welcomed her. She bathed her and perfumed her, and attired her in royal robes. She then made her tea, and lit her a water-pipe.

The girl then told the young man that he should go and ask the Sultan to visit him the next day. He did so, and the Sultan accepted.

On the following day, the Sultan arrived at their place, together with his grand judge and his Wazir.

After the youth had made them welcome, the girl came to sit with them and asked the Sultan, "Why did you have this woman wrapped in a camel-skin and punished?"

"Because she committed a vile deed," he replied.

The girl then asked for the mid-wife, and the two wives to be brought before the Sultan.

When these three were brought forth, the girl asked them what they knew about the third bride.

At first, the three denied any knowledge, but then the girl turned to the Sultan and the judge and declared, "This young man is your son from this woman. The black dogs were placed in his place by the mid-wife at the instigation of your two other wives, a deed for which they gave her one thousand Dinars." She told them where the money could be found.

The Sultan sent a policeman to the house of the mid-wife, where he found the money at the designated place.

When the king realised the evil deed perpetrated by his two wives and the mid-wife, he had their heads cut off, and took back the wife that he had so shamefully treated.

The girl and the Sultan's son, were joined in marriage, and lived together in happiness to the end of their days.

THE PUMPKIN

Once upon a time, there lived a very poor thorn-seller. Every day he ventured out into the desert to collect the desert thorn; brought it into Baghdad, and sold it in order it to buy bread for his children.

One day it rained heavily, and the thorn-seller said to his wife, "The rain is so heavy, and the weather is so cold. I do not think I will be able collect thorn today."

His wife replied, "But if you do not collect thorn, what will the little children eat?

The man said, "I will go out and see what I can find," and he went out into the rain and the mud with his axe slung over his shoulder. But he found no thorn to cut, for it was all wet and of no use as firewood. So he went into the alleys of Baghdad and began to search among the refuse which the stall-holders in the market had thrown away into the road.

He gathered some leaves and vegetables which had been thrown away. Among them lay a little dry-looking pumpkin which he picked up with the rest, saying to himself, "I will plant this in the ground. Perhaps it may become a useful plant."

His wife made a little soup, and fed the children that night. He put the dry pumpkin on a shelf in his room.

At midnight he woke, and he heard a voice calling him, "*Yaab*! *Yaab*! O father, O father!"

He answered, "*Eyn Yaab*! Who calls me father? "

The voice seemed to come from the shelf where he had put the pumpkin, and it said, "Take me to the daughter of the Sultan and marry her to me."

The thorn-seller could do nothing but laugh at the suggestion, and said, "How can a poor thorn-seller, like me, even look at the Sultan's palace, let alone approach it? How can I betroth you to the Sultan's daughter?"

The pumpkin said, "Open your *dishdasha*!"

As he opened his *dishdasha*, a hundred gold pieces came tumbling into it. The thorn-seller, who had never dreamt of so much money, was speechless and overjoyed.

He could not sleep that night. Early in the morning he went to the *suq* and bought bread, wheat, rice, meat, chickens, vegetables, and clothes for his children. He and his family rejoiced that day in a way they had never known.

That night he fell into a comfortable sleep. At midnight he was woken by a voice from the shelf. "*Yaab*! *Yaab*!"

And he replied, "*Eyn Yaab*! Who calls me father?"

And the pumpkin said, "Did you ask for the hand of the Sultan's daughter for me?"

The thorn-seller replied, "How could a poor thorn-seller, like me, ask the Sultan for his daughter? All I did was to buy food and clothes for my children."

The pumpkin said, "Open your *dishdasha*." And into the *dishdasha* of the thorn-seller there fell two hundred pieces of gold. And the pumpkin said, "Tomorrow go to the market and buy for yourself a fine mare and fine clothing and a servant. Then go to the palace of the Sultan and betroth me to his daughter!"

Early the next day, the thorn-seller bought the fine clothing, the mare and the slave and went to the Sultan's palace.

But the doorkeeper stopped him and said, "No one passes here without business as this is the Sultan's house!"

The thorn-seller said, "I know it is. I have business with the Sultan, I must speak with him about a personal matter."

The doorkeeper replied, "*Imshi*, go away! As you have no permit to enter the palace, I can't let you in!"

He returned home disappointed. That night he was woken again, by a voice. He heard the pumpkin say, "*Yaab! Yaab!*" and he answered, "*Eyn Yaab!*"

Then the pumpkin said, "Did you betroth me to the Sultan's daughter?"

And the thorn-seller said, "I went to the *suq*, and bought what you told me to buy and rode with the servant to the Sultan's palace. But they refused to let me in."

The pumpkin said, "Open your *dishdasha*!"

And into the thorn-sellers *dishdasha* there fell three hundred gold pieces. Then he said to him, "Tomorrow, when you get to the palace, push the doorkeeper aside without a word and go up the stairs. When you enter the *diwan* of the Sultan you will see two chairs, one of silver and one of gold. He who has a petition to make sits on the silver chair and he who is a suitor to the princess sits in the gold chair. Sit on the gold chair and speak boldly!"

The next day the thorn-seller put on his fine clothes, and rode his mare to the palace. When he got there he went up the stairs without saying a word to the keeper. On arriving at the *diwan*, he sat on the gold chair.

The Sultan, his court and his ministers were present. When the Sultan noticed him, he looked at him out of half his eye, and said to himself, "Who is this fellow who dares to ask for my daughter's hand?"

Then he spoke to the thorn-seller, "*Shaku indek*? What is your business?"

The thorn-seller answered, "I want your daughter as a wife for my son!"

The Sultan was furious and turned to his Wazir and said, "Who does he thinks he is to dare and ask for my daughter? I will cut off his head!"

The Wazir advised him that it was not proper of a ruler to act like this in such circumstances. It was wise, the Wazir thought, to place such heavy conditions on him which when fulfilled earned him the daughter. However, should he fail to fulfil them, he would stand to lose his head. The Sultan said, "*Zain*! Good."

Then he turned to the thorn-seller and said, "In the space of three days I want you to build a castle that will extend from your house to my palace. I want it to be built of gold bricks. The galleries and gallery posts should be of gold, and the door knobs of diamonds. The bedsteads I want made of gold, and the bedspreads of pearls and emeralds. The carpets should be embroidered with precious stones. If you build such a castle, your son shall marry my daughter. If you fail, I will cut off your head."

Although the thorn-seller said, "All right," he was terrified as he did not know what was awaiting him.

When his wife saw him like this, she asked him, "What is the matter with him?"

He told her that he expected to die following the conditions imposed by the Sultan. When she heard the whole story, she said, "Allah is merciful. Why not ask your son the pumpkin, perhaps he can help you. Ask him tonight."

That night the thorn-seller could not sleep. At midnight he heard the pumpkin cry, "*Yaab*! *Yaab*!" and answered, "*Eyn Yaab*!" and the pumpkin said, "Did you go to the Sultan and ask him for his daughter?"

The thorn-seller told him about his misfortune and his impending death as he would not be able to meet the conditions set out by the Sultan..

The son of the *jinn* who was in the pumpkin began to laugh. The thorn-seller cried, "How can you laugh when I watch death approaching me?"

He went on laughing and said, "What the Sultan has asked is nothing at all! It is easy! Open your *dishdasha*," and into the thorn-seller's *dishdasha* there fell four hundred gold pieces.

The pumpkin continued, "Do not worry any more, do not bother yourself with the Sultan's conditions."

The thorn-seller took the money and went to sleep. As he got up the next morning and found no castle when he looked out of the window, fear began to creep into heart. But the pumpkin had given him five hundred gold pieces and asked him not to worry.

The following morning there still was no castle to be seen. At night he was troubled, and wept, but the pumpkin gave him six hundred gold pieces and advised him to sleep and not be afraid as he was going to take care of everything.

On the third morning he woke to a golden light shining in his room. When he looked out, he saw a castle of bright gold stretching between his house and the Sultan's palace.

Meanwhile, in the palace the Sultan got up, and experienced the same golden light shining through his window. He looked out and saw the castle. When he entered it, he found everything better than he desired.

Then he sent for the thorn-seller, and said, "It shall be as you wish, today we will make the marriage contract." He sent for the *mullah*, and the contract was drawn up. The marriage was celebrated with festivities fitting for a Sultan in Baghdad.

That night, the thorn-seller told the pumpkin that the contract was made and the marriage was complete.

Then the pumpkin said, "Tell the Sultan that the bridegroom will come to the bride on Thursday. I shall come to her after the guests have departed. The door of the bridal chamber must be left open"

Festivities were made for Thursday. After the guests had all left, the princess was seated in the bridal chamber on a couch, alone, dressed gorgeously, and waiting.

At midnight a little bird flew in through the open door of the bridal chamber and sat on the bed, and in its claw was a stick.

The bird descended to the ground, and struck the stick on the floor, and took off its cloak of feathers, and grew, and behold! A handsome young man stood before her.

Then he struck the ground again and it opened. In the floor there appeared a large pool, and out of the water came forty beautiful young women, one carrying a towel embroidered with gold; another carrying a loofah; another a golden basin, another a golden comb, another *teen khawa,* another soap, another a massage-glove, another a bowl to hold the jewels, bath-towels, every one carried something.

Then they took off the bridegroom's clothes, and led him into the pool. They washed; perfumed him and put on his robe. Then they put him on the bedstead beside the bride and began to sing

When this was completed, he struck with his stick, and the young women went into the water, the pool disappeared, and the floor closed back as it was.

Then they made love and spent the night in sweetness and love.
He, then, said to her, "I want you to promise me to keep silent about me. Do not describe me, or say how I come to you. Do not say a word about me, or I will go away and you will never see me again."

She whispered, "I promise." And he put on his dress of feathers and flew away.

The next day was the *subhiya*, the Feast of the Next Day. Her friends and relations came to visit. The thorn-seller and his children came too. There was music and feasting in honour of the married pair.

They asked her, "*Shloaneh*? How was the bridegroom?" They were all keen to know something about him.
She only answered, "Praise be to Allah.

For two years the bridegroom came to her every night. They enjoyed each other's company and she could not have been happier. But one day she said to her attendant, "I want to go to the *hammam* in the *suq*."

Answered the handmaid, "O my daughter, why go to the *suq*, when you have a more beautiful *hammam* here?"

She answered, "But I wish to go outside and have some change. Going to the public bath is a good change."

As she insisted the handmaid gathered all her bath things, and they both went to the bath. When the princess entered, all the women there greeted her, and she sat in a corner. The women began to whisper about her maliciously and said, "Every one knows she is married to a sparrow!"

She heard their whispering, and was angry. Unable to restrain herself she cried out, "My husband is not a sparrow! He is a normal man, like other men."

As she said this, the sparrow flew down through the hole in the dome of the bath and perched on her shoulder. "Did I not have your promise not to say anything about me?" He said. "Now you will never see me again". Then he seized her golden comb and her bracelet, and flew away.

She wept and lamented. Her tears ran in streams down her face.

The wife of the thorn-seller came to the castle to console her and said, "My darling, do not weep! Allah is merciful. Perhaps he will come again!" But that did not help her, as she felt her loss was too great to be consoled by words.

A year passed during which the princess mourned her husband as if he were dead. Then she said to herself, "I must set myself something to do." So she called an *'usta,* a skilled labourer, and ordered him, "Build me a *hammam* in the shortest time possible."

He nodded, "Aye, I will."

He and his fellows worked, and in two weeks they had built a fine bathhouse. When it was complete, the princess put a notice on the door saying that the lady who told her a story would be permitted to bathe for free.

She hoped that that if every one who came to the bath told a tale, she might hear something about her missing husband.

So she sat on a chair at the door of the bath, guarding the jewellery and possessions of the bathers, and they paid her by telling her a story.

One day an old, dirty woman came to the bath. She said to the princess, "O honourable princess, I wish to wash. My head is very dirty."

The princess said, "You may wash for free, if you tell me a story."

The old woman knew no story, so she said, "Many thanks, O princess! I will go away now, and wash my dirty clothes in the river first, and buy myself a little soap and return tomorrow to wash my head."

The old woman returned to her house. At sunrise she got up and walked towards the river to wash her clothes. When she got there, she washed them and put them next to her to dry.

As she sat there, she saw a bird come out of the water with two water-skins on his back. He swam to the edge; filled his skins and dived into the water again.

The old woman was amazed, and said to herself, "If he comes up again, I will catch him by the tail!" He appeared again, and as he finished filling the skins, the old woman caught hold of him by the tail. He dived underneath the water, and as she clung on to him tightly, she also went under.

Under the water, they came to a beautiful castle. In front of the castle there was a pool of water and near the pool was a long table, set for forty diners.

She thought to herself that this would make a good tale for the princess, but first she wanted to see all that there was to be seen. So she entered the castle and came to the kitchen. There, on the fire, were fish and meat cooking, but there was no one there. Dishes were being taken to the table outside, but she could see no one carrying them, they moved in the air.

She stretched out her hand to eat out of a dish, but was soon struck on her hand and a voice cried,
Jurri idech
Take your hand away!
Sidi me yahibbech wa la yaridech
My master doesn't love you and doesn't want you!

She withdrew her hand immediately.

Then she thought to herself, "I will hide under the couch to see who is coming to eat." So she hid herself below the couch. Soon she saw forty doves fly down. Forty fair damsels came up out of the pool to meet them, each bearing towel, bathing wraps, soap, friction gloves, and everything necessary for the bath.

The doves took off their dresses of feathers, and there stood forty beautiful youths. The youths dived into the pool; were washed; dried and clothed. They sat at the table to eat. Soon the food appeared, and after they had finished, they washed their hands and mouths. Then each arose and went into the castle and entered his own room.

The old woman thought to herself, "I must go and see what is in these rooms." So she followed them and went up the stairs. She entered the rooms and saw the first of the forty youths reading a book, another sleeping, another writing. Each was doing something or just sleeping.

When she came to the fortieth room and looked in, she saw the youth sitting at a table and on his knees were some bracelets and a golden comb. He was sighing, with tears running down his face, and saying:

Ya dar, ya dar!
O house! O house!
Abchi 'al umm el mikhashkhash wils swar!
I weep for the lady of the anklets and bracelets!

The old woman said to herself, "This must be the missing husband of the princess who keeps the bath."

Fearing that she might not be able to return to the world above, she rushed to the place where the bird had left her. He came with two skins on his back. She seized his tail and he flew up through the water and arrived at the bank.

It was already dawn. The old woman picked up her clothes, and thought that she had a wonderful story to tell the princess. She bought a bar of soap and went to the bath.

The old woman said to the princess, "I have a fine story to tell you, the like of which you have never heard."

The princess could not wait any longer and asked her to tell it at once. The old woman recounted what had happened in the river and what she had seen.

When she had finished the princess embraced her, and ordered the bath attendants to take the old woman and wash her well, and give her fine new clothes.

When this was done, they brought her back to the princess. Then the princess said, "You must come back to my house, so that tonight you can take me to the young man who has my bracelets." The old woman readily agreed.

At night, when it was dark, the old woman said, "Let us go, my daughter," and they went to the river bank and waited. At midnight there came the bird, and the old woman said, "When I catch hold of his tail, you hold on to my dress."

The girl did as she was told; when the bird had filled his water-skins, the old woman held his tail and the princess did as she had been told, and they went through the water to the pool and the castle.

The table was spread as it was on the previous night, and the old woman and the princess went into the kitchen and saw food cooking and dishes being carried in the air to the table outside.

The princess stretched out her hand and put it into one of the dishes, and a voice cried:

177

Middi eedich, middi eedich
Stretch your hand, stretch your hand!
Sidi yehibbich wee reedich
My master loves you and wants you!

So she picked the food and ate it.

Then the old woman said to her, "We must hide beneath the couch."

So they hid beneath the couch, and all that had happened the previous night happened again.

When she saw her husband, the princess could not restrain herself, and said to the old woman, "That is my husband, that is him."

When the forty sons of the *jinn* had eaten; washed their hands and mouths, they then went up the steps of the castle, each to his own chamber.

The old woman and the Sultan's daughter followed them, and looked into each room. As they came to the fortieth room, they saw the princess's husband, weeping, and on his knee lay the bracelet and the golden comb.

The old woman said to him, "If you really want her? I will bring her to you!" And the young man said, "You are a human, how have you dared to enter our house?" The old woman replied,

"Allah brought me here, so that I may bring your wife to you."

"My wife!" He said, "Where is my wife?"

"Here!" When he saw her he jumped up and embraced her.

Then he said to her, "You must leave now because my brothers and sisters will kill you if they find you here. I will return to you as a man and will not leave you again."

They then, holding on to the bird's his tail, were flown to the shore of the river. The next night there was a knock at the door of the princess's house. When she opened, there was her husband, a normal man. Although he was the son of the Sultan of the *jinn*, he remained with her, a human husband.

THE PORTER AND THE THIEVES

Once upon a time, in the city of Basra, there lived a woman who was married to a very simple-minded poor *hammal*, porter. She was unsatisfied with her lot, and she blamed her husband for their poverty. She used to beat him and lock him out of the house whenever it pleased her. One day she beat him and told him to go out and bring her the jewels of the Wazir's wife.

He went to sleep on a bench in a *gahwa*, coffee shop. A band of seven thieves passed by and asked him what was he doing, sleeping there. He said, "My wife beat me and ordered me to go and get her the jewels of the Wazir's wife."

The seven thieves told him that, rather than sleep the night in the *gahwa,* he could join them as a helper in their next robbery. He did not have to do anything except assist in carrying the booty.

When they reached their target; the seven thieves told the porter to sit tight and make no noise while they went and emptied the wardrobes and cupboards. The porter, however, got tired of waiting. He went upstairs and decided to stretch his legs by walking on the roof .

He saw the owner of the house and his wife sleeping under a fine quilt. (It is the custom of the people of Iraq to sleep on the rooftops in summer). It was a finely decorated quilt which looked very beautiful in the moonlight.

181

The porter thought to himself that if he were to take that beautiful quilt to his wife, she might take him back and treat him kindly.

He took the quilt from the sleeping couple, but then his conscience pricked him; he thought that the couple would catch a cold if left without a quilt and so decided to go downstairs and bring a replacement quilt for them.

As he was about to cover them, the couple woke up and asked him in anguish, "Who are you? What are you doing here?"

The porter replied, "I am an assistant thief."

"An assistant thief! What are you doing here?"

The porter then told them the whole story starting with his cruel wife who had thrown him out and how the thieves had found him and asked him to help them.

He explained that he thought that his wife would take him back if he took their fine quilt to her, but he could not let them catch a cold while sleeping without cover. That was the reason why he came back to cover them.

"Where are the seven thieves?" Asked the man.

"They are downstairs collecting the fine things in your house," replied the porter.

As the couple rushed downstairs, the thieves fled. The couple found their jewels and fine items collected in the centre of the house. They kept the porter for the rest of the night and in the morning they thanked him for saving their house and gave him the red quilt as a reward.

The porter went home very pleased with himself and said, "Wife, come and see this fine quilt that I have brought you."

His wife took the quilt from him, and said, "*Kelb ibnel kelb*, Dog, son of a dog, I wanted you to bring me the jewels of the Wazir's wife and you bring me this simple quilt. Get out and do not come back until you have brought the jewels."

The porter went to the coffee shop again to spend the night. The band of seven thieves passed by again. Their leader said, "You, dog, son of a dog. What did you do to us yesterday? You deserve to be killed for that."

But the other thieves pleaded with him to spare his life for being such a simple-minded man. The leader refused to accept their intercession.

The other six persisted, "Let us give him another chance. We take him along tonight as our helper. Forgive him for being such a stupid man." Finally their leader relented and agreed to give him another chance.

They took the porter with them again to the house targeted for robbery, and before they entered the house told him to sit tight and not to leave his spot until they summoned him.

The thieves broke into the house; entered the room; cleared out all the valuables; and bundled them together and were ready to leave with the booty.

In the meantime, while sitting there, the porter saw a shining copper bucket by the well. He thought to himself that if he took the beautiful bucket to his wife to replace the old jar they had at home, then maybe she would take him and treat him with kindness.

He noticed, however, that the cistern was empty and thought that now that he was taking the bucket away, he could at least fill the cistern for them. He set out to do so. As he began to lower the bucket into the well, the pulleys squeaked. He kept lowering and raising filling the bucket in order to fill the cistern. The squeaking noise was so high-pitched that the occupants of the house woke up.

When they came to the courtyard they caught the porter and asked him, "What are you doing?"

He answered, "*Wallah*, there were seven thieves here but they have fled. I am only an assistant thief: They brought me here as a helper to carry the booty. My wife has thrown me out of the house until I bring her the jewels of the Wazir's wife, but I thought this bucket will make her take me back. I felt sorry for leaving you with an empty cistern.".

They thanked him for having saved them from the robbers and kept him till the morning. Then they gave him the copper bucket and sent him home.

When he got home he knocked on the door and called out, "O wife, come and see the wonderful bucket I have brought you."

She said, taking the bucket away, "Get out. I asked you to bring me the jewels of the Wazir's wife and you bring me this simple bucket. Do not come back unless you have her jewels".

When night fell again, the porter went to sleep on the bench in the coffee shop, and as the seven thieves passed, their leader said, " *Gawwad,* You pimp,! Tonight I will surely kill you."

The other thieves again pleaded for the porter as they had the night before and the leader relented and pardoned him.

They took him along with them to their new target for robbery that night and ordered him to sit tight. They broke into the house as they had done the previous two nights and started to collect the valuable items.

As the porter sat in the spot allocated for him he saw a shining brass mortar and pestle. He thought, what a change it would make from their old iron mortar and pestle.

Perhaps if he took it to his wife, she would love him and take him back. As he was removing it he noticed some cardamom seeds in the mortar not yet crushed.

He thought, "If I took away their mortar how will they crush their cardamom seeds tomorrow. Let me crush them before I leave."

The noise of crushing the seeds woke up the occupants of the house and caused the thieves to flee.

The people of the house shouted, "Who is that?"

He said, "I....I am an assistant thief."

He explained to them everything that had happened, as he had done in the two previous nights. They were grateful for him because he

185

had saved their house from theft. They kept him till morning and then gave him the mortar and pestle and sent him home.

His wife took the mortar and pestle; cursed him; beat him and threw him out telling him not to come back without the jewels of the Wazir's wife.

The porter thought to himself, "If I sleep again on the bench in the coffee shop the thieves will surely kill me this time. *Weyn arooh*! Where shall I go!"

He went to a friend and borrowed a flute. He thought that if he played some music he would make some money to pay for the cost of his night. So he went through the streets playing the flute asking for payment for his entertaining playing.

By night he found himself near the open door of the Wazir's palace. The palace was, as usual in palaces of those days, divided into two parts, one for the men and one for the women. Close to the door was a storeroom for straw. The porter slipped in and immediately climbed up on top of the straw. As soon as he got there he fell asleep.

The Wazir's wife had a lover who came to her every night when the Wazir was fast asleep. They met in the straw room for their affair.

"Why were you late tonight?" She quietly asked. He said, "I was at a wedding party and couldn't leave and come until now." She brought him a stuffed chicken and rice.

"Did you dance?" asked she. "Yes, every one had to dance in turn".

"I would love to see you dance", she said.

"But how can you see me in the dark?" She said, "I will bring some light to see you dance."

By that time the porter was awakened by the noise and the smell of food. He stretched out his hand and guided by his senses reached for the chicken; grabbed it and started to eat it.

When the Wazir's wife returned with the light her lover said, "Why did you give me only rice?"

"No, *habibi,* I brought chicken with the rice. Maybe a cat has stolen it", she said. The woman began to snap her fingers and said, "Let me see you dance a little".

The porter thought it would be nice if he joined in and played some music to assist the lover in his dancing. As soon as he started to play his flute, the lover was out of the room in no time.

The Wazir's wife thought that there was a *jinni* in the room. She said, "Please *jinni*, do not wake my husband up."

"I will only be quiet if you give me your jewels," he said while still playing his flute.

"You can have all of my jewels if you stop. I will go and fetch them." She rushed and brought her jewel box with all her jewels in it.

The porter reached his house before dawn and he knocked on the door, with delight. "Who is it?" asked his wife.

"It is I! Open the door. I have brought you what you have always wanted ."

The wife opened the door and took the box and found golden ornaments for the neck, the wrist, the ears and the fingers. This time the wife let her husband stay with her. She sold some of the jewels in order to buy a better house and lived there in peace with her poor husband.

THE JINNI OF THE WELL

There lived once a very poor old man in a village near the city of Mosul. He worked hard all his life but achieved nothing and did not even cover his basic needs to the extent that he and his wife had to beg.

To add to his misery his wife had a devilish tongue which afflicted him day and night. On one of those unfortunate days, when they had nothing to eat, she began to abuse and scold him and saying, "Here we are starving, and you sit on your backside doing nothing! There has never been a woman, like me, so cursed with such a bum as you!"

He was forced to go out to seek work. He went on searching for work, but no man would employ him as the harvest season was over. He sat down by the roadside and reflected on how his wife would treat him if he went home with no income.

It was then full noon, and as he sat watching the wheel-marks and people flowing over the hill, he thought to himself, "Mosul is a beautiful city, and if Allah so willed it maybe wealth awaits us there". But suddenly he realised that no money would be worth anything if his wife was to continue to plague him. He decided to go to Mosul alone.

With this clear thought in his mind he felt joy. With a piece of bread in his mouth, he rose up and set out upon the road. He walked until he came upon a well and a shady tree, where he decided to refresh himself, and to sit on the edge of the well to rest.

He had only rested a little when he saw on the brow of the hill a cloud of dust. As it came nearer, he could see that it was caused by a woman, and not just any woman, but his scolding wife. As soon as she was within earshot, she began to curse and abuse him for deserting her, calling him a dog and *Kelb ibnel kelb,* a son of a dog, *Naghal,* the child of iniquity, eater of filth, and a doer of evil.

He did not say a word as she sat next to him on the edge of the well reviling. She went on doing this until he lost patience and pushed her with his elbow into the well below. He was frightened, but deep down he was happy to be got rid of her. Regardless of her screams, he went on his way. It was by the will of Allah that he was a free man after forty years of suffering.

It was nearing sunset, when he stopped to prepare himself for the evening prayer. But there in the distance he saw a cloud of dust, coming nearer and nearer. As it came nearer, he could see that this time it was not his wife, but a *jinni*, who approached him angrily and cried, "I have come to kill you!"

The old man fell on his knees begging, "What have I done, O *Emir* of the *jinn*, that earned me your anger? Will you give me time to say my prayers, and then tell me your reasons for wanting to kill me."

"Don't I have reasons to be angry?" Shouted the *jinni*. "For forty years I have lived peacefully in my well, until today when you cast into it a woman whose tongue is a plague and her screaming like the screaming of peacocks!"

The old man responded, "O prince of the *jinn*, for forty years you have had peace and for only two hours a woman's tongue. But what of my miserable luck? For forty years I have had this woman's tongue, and only for two hours have I had peace and quietness. Have mercy on me, may Allah bless you with his mercy."

"You, indeed, have been unlucky", commiserated the *jinni*, "but what shall we do to the woman in my well?"

"O *Emir* of the *jinn*, leave her there and let us travel the world together."

The *jinni* was pleased with the suggestion made by the old man and together they travelled until they reached Mosul. There they sought shelter in a *khan* and ordered the best that could be provided for them.

The *jinni* paid for all the costs, and the next day he bought a large house with many servants. There he and the old man lived together, entertaining the notables of the town and spending lavishly.

A time came when the *jinni* became restless with this kind of life, and he said to the old man, "If we continue to live together I will do you harm. It is better if we part now."

"But without money what shall I do?" Asked the old man.

"I will show you how to become rich and famous," said the *jinni*. "I enjoy entering people's minds and making them mad. When I part with you, I shall enter the mind of the daughter of the Wazir of Baghdad. He will pay anything for the man who could cure the possessed girl, and that man will be you."

"But how do I know how to cure her?" asked the old man.

"I will tell you how on one condition - that you do not again employ exorcism against me. Because if you do, I will enter into your head and never leave you." He then taught the old man the art of exorcism.

Thereafter he disappeared, and the old man left Mosul and travelled to Baghdad. Shortly after he had resided in Baghdad, he heard the news that the Wazir's daughter was grievously ill and that a *jinni* had entered into her head and was tormenting her.

The old man went to the Wazir's palace and informed the servants that he was a skilled physician with special skill in curing those possessed. The Wazir, after being informed, received him and enquired if he, indeed, could cure his daughter. The old man said, "O Highness, I can cure her, but not without my just reward."

"What do you expect as a reward?" Asked the Wazir.

The old man answered, "My price is ten thousand dinars."

When the Wazir heard this figure, he was very angry. "This demand is, indeed, beyond reason," cried the Wazir. "Are you the only doctor in Baghdad to demand such an exorbitant sum?"

He sent the old man away. But day by day his daughter's situation worsened and the doctors and exorcists exhausted their means.

Every treatment known in Baghdad was tried. She was conducted to the shrine of *Abdul Qader al Gailani*, and left there for three days and nights. She was chained to the grill at the tomb of the two

Khadims for yet another such period. The *Qur'an* was repeatedly read over her. She was given magic potions to drink, and was beaten to the point of death, but all in vain.

Then the old man went again to the Wazir and told him that he was able and willing to cure his daughter. "Cure her," cried the Wazir, "and I will pay your price, even the ten thousand dinars."

"O Wazir," said the old man, "my price is different now. It is now one-half of all your possessions!"

The Wazir was enraged at this demand and swore that he would not give it.

He said, "I don't need you because today a wise man from India is arriving, and by the will of Allah, he will cure her!" "Let it be as you desire," said the old man as he left.

But the wise man from India failed to cure the Wazir's daughter. Then the Wazir, in desperation, sent for the old man and pleaded with him, "O wise man, cure my daughter, and I will give you half of what I possess."

"O Wazir," said the old man, "my price has changed. It is now half of your possessions and the hand of your daughter."

"Take what you ask if the cure works", said the Wazir and he warned, "But if there is no cure, take care, you will lose your head."

The old man was then taken to the room where the Wazir's daughter was chained. As he was left alone with her, he pronounced the word of power which the *jinni* had taught him. A loud scream was heard as the evil spirit departed from her.

The maiden blushed at finding herself alone with a strange man, but when he told her that he was her deliverer and future husband, she greeted him with kindness and permitted him to cut her chains. Then they went to her father, who was overjoyed to see her back to normal. So there were marriage festivities lasting seven days and seven nights. The old man found his lost youth in his beautiful bride. He lived happily with her for a few months.

One day, while sitting at home, the old man received a message from his father-in-law, bidding him come at once to his palace.

He went, and the Wazir received him, saying to him in anguish, "The Khalifa, has ordered me to bring you to his palace without delay. His favourite daughter is being possessed by a terrible *jinni*."

The old man was afraid that this might be the same *jinni* of the well. He tried to excuse himself from accompanying the Wazir, but the Wazir would not have any of this, and insisted that they must obey the commands of the Khalifa.

When they arrived in the presence of the Khalifa, the old man kissed the ground, and when he ordered to visit the princess, he said, "O Commander of the Faithful, I am but a poor man with little knowledge. Why not send for your physicians and let them heal the princess."

The Khalifa became enraged and said, "What is the meaning of this? Why are you unwilling to exercise upon my daughter the skill which you have proven upon the family of my Wazir?"

The old man said, "Not because of unwillingness, but from my incapacity to handle such a task."

"I don't want to hear any lies!" Cried the Khalifa. "Does not all Baghdad know you for a skilled exorcist after having succeeded in expelling a demon from the daughter of my Wazir? Why are you making such excuses? Cure my daughter, or by Allah, I will hand you over to the executioner at once".

Then he ordered the old man be taken to the quarters of the princess.

As the old man was being led through the palace towards the women's quarters, he beat his breast and wept bitterly. "*Aweylakh!* What man can run away from his fate? I have no choice but a terrible death or a life of torment."

He arrived to see the sick princess on her bed gazing widely with open eyes. He stood there with the hand of the executioner on his shoulder, and thought of the lovely bride he had just left behind.

In a few seconds he reviewed all the disappointments of his miserable life, beginning with his first marriage. He then bit on his hand, and cried, "What a *Booma*, an owl, am I!" And hope, which a moment before had flown from him, returned to his breast.

As he approached the princess, he pronounced the word the *jinni* had taught him.

Suddenly the evil *jinni* leapt from her body, and got hold of the old man crying, "You fool! What did I warn you not to do! Now I shall enter into your body and torment you until you die!"

"O *Emir* of the *jinn*," answered the old man, "Enter my body as you please, because one torment is not worse than the other. Did you know that my wife has escaped from the well and is waiting outside for me."

"What!" cried the *jinni*, "Live next to your wife and listen to her tongue? Never, never!" And with a loud cry he flew to the window and leapt from it into the air and was never seen or heard of in that land afterwards.

Thus ends the story of the *jinni* of the well.

LEELU

Kann ya ma kann, It was and was not.
Wa 'ala Allah at tuklan. Our reliance is upon Allah.

There lived long ago in the thriving port city of Basra a merchant who had three daughters. One day, he had to travel to a far off land for business. When he was getting ready he asked his eldest daughter, "Darling daughter, what do you want me to bring you from my journey?"

She said, "*Salamtek*! your safety and a pretty dress."

Similarly, he asked the second daughter who responded, "*Salamtek*! your safety and a pretty dress too."

Then he turned to the youngest daughter, and asked her the same. Not knowing much about material things, she rushed to her mother and asked, "*Mama*, what shall I ask *Baba* to bring me when he returns from his journey?"

The mother said, "Ask for *Leelu,* pearls"

So she went to her father and said, "I want a cluster of *Leelu*."

The father promised all his daughters to bring them back what they had asked, and then he sailed to the distant land. When he finished the business he had travelled for, he went to the *suq*, and he bought two lengths of fine silk for his two eldest daughters, but he forgot all about the youngest's gift. He loaded his goods onto the ship and embarked.

The captain went around the ship giving the same message to all passengers, "Have you finished all your business? This ship will not sail if any business is unfinished or anything is left undone."

When he put it to the father, the latter suddenly remembered that he had forgotten to buy the *Leelu* for his youngest daughter. When he informed the captain, he told him that the ship would await his return from the shore as he went to buy the present for his youngest daughter.

The merchant went ashore again, and went to the *suq* of the jewellers and said, "I wish to buy *Leelu*."

The merchants in the *suq* told him, "Leelu is the name of the son of the Sultan of the *jinn*."

He asked them, "Where is this Leelu to be found?"

They directed him to the place where the Sultan of the *jinn* lived. The merchant went to the palace of the Sultan and knocked on the door.

A voice from inside the palace asked, "Who is it at the door?"

The merchant answered, "I."
The voice said, "What do you want?

He said, "Leelu."

As the door opened, there stood before him a handsome young man who said to him, "I am Leelu. What is it that you want of me?"

The merchant said, "When I left my country to come here, I promised each one of my three daughters the present of her choice. To the two eldest, I promised new dresses, and to the youngest, I promised *Leelu*."

Leelu said to the merchant, "First you must build your daughter a new bare room; give to her this box which has three hairs inside it, and tell her to sit in the centre of the room and to rub the three hairs together. Whatever she sees after that she must not utter a word or a cry but simply exclaim *Mashallah,* what Allah willed, thrice."

The merchant bid the boy farewell and sailed until he got home. He was warmly greeted by his wife and daughters. After he sat down and relaxed for a while, the daughters were eager to have their presents. The father then opened his trunks and gave his two eldest daughters their dresses.

When the youngest asked, "Where is my Leelu?" He replied, "My darling daughter, I really forgot what you asked for, so I have brought you nothing."

That night he could not sleep easily. He turned to his wife and told her the story of Leelu, the son of the Sultan of the *jinn.* Then he asked her if she thought he should build the room for the daughter as Leelu instructed and leave her alone in it. He was not able to decide on his own and sought his wife's advice on this matter.

His wife answered him, "Build it. I can see good fortune for our daughter coming from it."

Next morning the merchant ordered builders to build a new room, and the threshold was left bare as Leelu had ordered. When the room was finished, the young daughter was bathed, finely dressed and then led by her father and mother into the room. There her father gave her the box and instructed her to rub the three hairs together, but utter nothing except *Mashallah*, three times.

When the girl was alone, she rubbed the three hairs together as her father instructed her and waited. She saw the threshold becoming a lake and upon the lake swam a ship of crystal. As the ship approached her, she saw in it a boy,

Subhan Allah al khaliq, wal khaliq ahsan!
Praise to Allah who created him,
and the Creator is better than his creation!

The young daughter was amazed, but she said no words but *Mashallah*, three times.

The boy then disembarked, embraced her and kissed her. They spent that night together in happiness.

In the morning he told her, "If anything should happen to part us, then you should go and look for me. You must put on a shoe of iron and carry an iron staff". He instructed her not to say a word about what happened that night and departed. The ship disappeared, the lake evaporated and the threshold became as it was.

When her parents came to her all that she told them was that she was happy. That night she did what she did the night before. She went on doing this for many nights spending them in happiness with Leelu.

The eldest sister guessed that something was happening especially as she saw her sister so happy. Blinded by jealousy, she decided to act.

When the family next went to the bath, the eldest daughter refused to bathe saying she was not feeling well. As the rest of the family undressed and went inside, she went to her youngest sister's clothes and stole the key to the room from her pocket.

She rushed home and went straight to the room, unlocked it and seated herself in her sister's place. She opened the box, picked the three hairs and rubbed them together.

The lake and the crystal ship appeared. When she saw Leelu, she was overwhelmed and cried loudly with excitement. As she did this, the ship broke into splinters and entered the body of the boy. Then he and the lake disappeared, and she found herself back in the room.

The eldest daughter was terrified at what had happened. She ran out of the room and locked the door. When the rest of the family came back from the bath, she put the key back in her sister's pocket, and said nothing about it to anybody.

That night, when the young daughter went to the room and rubbed the hairs, nothing happened. She waited all night but nothing happened. She cried and cried. She was convinced that her envious sister had done something to harm her.

Next morning she went to her father, and told him that he must make her a pair of iron shoes and an iron staff, as she wanted to go and look for Leelu.

She travelled, and travelled, up and down valleys and over deserts. Finally she reached the outskirts of a town and she decided to rest after her exhausting journey. She sat beneath a large tree and closed her eyes.

On the boughs of this tree there were two doves cooing to each other. The girl heard their words and kept her eyes closed, but she listened with utmost concentration. This was what she heard:

"This girl fell in love with the son of the Sultan of the *jinn*. One day when she was at the bath, her jealous sister sneaked into her room and rubbed the three hairs together. When she saw the wonderful boy, she screamed with amazement. The ship broke into splinters which went into the body of the boy. When this girl came to call him, she got no response. She grieved so much for his loss that now she has come to look for him."

Then the other dove continued, "Now that boy is dying. His father has exhausted all means to cure him. But if the girl down there is awake she can cure him. She needs to seize us, kill us and take our blood and feathers and some of these leaves. She should then go to the palace of the Sultan of the *jinn* and cry outside that 'I am a healer'. When she is let in, she should take the boy to the bath; smear his body with our blood and feathers and then wipe it with the leaves. He will then be cured."

The girl jumped quickly and seized the two doves; she wrung their necks and poured their blood into her drinking cup. She then plucked their feathers and placed them in her handkerchief.

She cut some leaves from the tree and went towards the palace of the Sultan of the *jinn*.

When the Sultan of the *jinn* heard her crying, "I am a healer", he summoned her inside. The Sultan was desperate to try anything to cure his dying son, and so when the girl told him that she could cure his son if he was brought to the bath and left with her, he had him brought to her.

When she was alone with him, she took off his clothes, and dipped the feathers in the blood and smeared it all over his body. All the crystal splinters fell out of his body. She wiped his skin with the leaves, and his wounds closed and his flesh was healed. When he opened his eyes he did not recognise her and she was in a man's disguise.

She told him who she was and he was overjoyed at having been cured and united with her. He took her to his father, the Sultan, who, after hearing the whole story, said, "*Ya Bint Adam*, Daughter of man, as you have saved my son, you shall marry him and dwell with us in our land."

The wedding festivities went on for a full week. The boy and girl were married, and lived for the rest of their days happily in the land of the *jinn*.